D0977221

Caging the Nuclear Genie

NATIONAL UNIVERSITY
LIBRARY   SAN DIEGO

Caging the Nuclear Genie

An American Challenge for Global Security

Stansfield Turner

 WestviewPress

A Division of HarperCollins*Publishers*

All rights reserved. Printed in the United States of America. No part of this publication may be reproduced or transmitted in any form or by any means, electronic or mechanical, including photocopy, recording, or any information storage and retrieval system, without permission in writing from the publisher.

Copyright © 1997 by Westview Press, A Division of HarperCollins Publishers, Inc.

Published in 1997 in the United States of America by Westview Press, 5500 Central Avenue, Boulder, Colorado 80301-2877, and in the United Kingdom by Westview Press, 12 Hid's Copse Road, Cumnor Hill, Oxford OX2 9JJ

Library of Congress Cataloging-in-Publication Data
Turner, Stansfield, 1923–
    Caging the nuclear genie : an American challenge for global
security / Stansfield Turner.
        p.   cm.
    Includes index.
    ISBN 0-8133-3328-8
    1. No first use (Nuclear strategy)   2. Security, International.
I. Title.
U264.T87   1997
327.1'747—dc21   97-19178
                                                                                         CIP

The paper used in this publication meets the requirements of the American National Standard for Permanence of Paper for Printed Library Materials Z39.48-1984.

10   9   8   7   6   5   4   3   2   1

In memory of my parents, Wilhelmina and Oliver,
whose gift of example and whose love and encouragement
gave me the confidence always to reach a little higher;
and to my brother Twain, whose shortness of life forced me
to search for deeper meaning in my own.

CONTENTS

ACKNOWLEDGMENTS

This book would not have been feasible without generous grants from the Carnegie Corporation of New York. In addition to being most grateful for that support, I am appreciative of the advice and encouragement there of David Speedie and the late McGeorge Bundy. "Mac's" seminal work in the area of nuclear weapons was a constant guide and benchmark.

I am also very grateful to the W. Alton Jones Foundation for the grant that gave this project its initial momentum and to George Perkovich for his helpful advice from beginning to end.

The Norwegian Nobel Institute of Peace kindly provided me a Senior Research Fellowship and a stimulating environment in which to pursue this effort for six months. They assembled a diverse group to critique the work in progress, including Christoph Bertram of Hamburg and Pavel Baeev of Moscow. Geir Lundestad and Odd Arne Westad of the Institute offered helpful comments throughout my stay in Oslo.

John Chipman and Rose Gottemoeller of the International Institute of Strategic Studies in London were generous in bringing together a seminar to review an extended outline of the book. That group included some of the most prominent thinkers in this area, including Sir Michael Howard and Lawrence Freedman. I am most grateful to all of them for taking so much of their time.

The Peace Research Institute of Oslo also was kind in organizing a helpful seminar discussion that included Magne Barthe, Nils Petter Gleditsch, and Robert Bathurst.

I have been fortunate in having had assistance with research from a number of individuals during a span of four years. Hanno Kirk, Howard Diamond, Matt Didaleusky, and Jason Pate were able to devote the most time to it and were invaluable both for the facts they uncovered and the advice they proffered. Kurt Wendt, Zach Patrick, Milton Leitenberg, Garrett Ogden, Alex Slesar, and Peter Copeland also provided wonderful support.

Many individuals were kind enough to meet with me and offer suggestions: Robert McNamara, Bill Perry, and Dick Cheney, former secretaries of defense; Admiral Henry Chiles, then commander in chief of the U.S. Strategic Command; General Lee Butler, former commander in chief of the U.S. Strategic Command; Michael Nacht, Al Lieberman, and Fred Nyland of the U.S. Arms Control and Disarmament Agency; Janne Nolan, John Steinbrunner, Bill Kauffman, and Bruce Blair of the Brookings Institution; Roger Molander, Bruno Augenstein, and Jim Digby of the RAND Corporation; Robert Piacesi and Paul Garvin of G&P Associates, Inc.; Sergei Rogov of the Institute of the USA and Canada Studies in Moscow; James Jacobs of the Federal Emergency Management Agency; Steve Hadley, formerly of the Department of Defense; Bruce Russett and Gaddis Smith of Yale University; Father Brian Hehir of Harvard University; Brigadier Generals Jim Mathers and Lance Lord and Colonels Bob Kehler and Jack Byrnes of the U.S. Space Command; Major General Gary Curtin and Brigadier General Thomas Neary of the U.S. Strategic Command; Admiral Elmo Zumwalt, former chief of naval operations; Fred Ikle, Zbigniew Brzezinski, and Michael Mazaar of the Center for Strategic and International Studies; Harald Müller of the Peace Research Institute Frankfurt; Spurgeon Keeny of the Arms Control Association; George Questor, Mancur Olson, Thomas Schelling, Ivo Daalder, and Steve Fetter of the University of Maryland; Colonel Ronald Williams of the Defense Special Weapons Agency; and Andrew Marshall and Frank Miller of the U.S. Department of Defense. I am particularly indebted to President Carter not only for his spending time to give me very important advice on the thrust of the book but for reading and commenting on portions of it.

Ted Postol of MIT not only tutored me on the lethality of nuclear weapons but also did numerous calculations at my request. Kosta Tsipis, also of MIT, provided invaluable advice as to my use of the study he directed, "Nuclear Crash—The U.S. Economy After Small Nuclear Attacks."

I imposed upon many friends to read and make suggestions on various drafts. Their assistance in this was invaluable, both because they agreed and because they disagreed: Robert Monroe, Donald Rivkin, John Keeley, John Kieley, Ken Pollack, John Lewis Gaddis, Louis Halle, Robert O'Connell, John Rhinelander, Alton Frye, Eliot Cohen, Forrest Morgan, David

Bradley, Richard Harza, Jeffrey Zink, Ove and Sjur Tjelta, George Thibault, Nordau Goodman, Stevan Dedijer, Mike Pocalyko, John Holdren, David Tall, Alvin Weinberg, Frank Tatum, Felix Moos, Staser Holcomb, Steve Nichalson, Alan Cranston, Charles Battaglia, David Rosenberg, Winn Price, William Karzas, Paul Grimes, Roger Ingle, Lynn Eden, and John Opel. I have been overwhelmed by this outpouring of support for finding ways to grapple with the vexing issues that nuclear weapons present. Having been shameless in asking for such assistance, I apologize if I have inadvertently overlooked someone upon whom I imposed.

Fran Burwell and Andrea White of the Center for International and Security Studies at Maryland rendered wonderful assistance and advice in administering the grants.

My assistant, Patricia Moynihan, had been through this twice before with me and was just as wonderfully patient, exacting, and efficient.

My wife, Eli Karin, was not only my constant adviser and supporter but also my editor until the manuscript was turned over to Westview Press. Her ability to unravel my syntax in a language that is not her native one is superb. At Westview Press, Peter Kracht was wonderfully sympathetic and helpful.

None of the supporting individuals or foundations, of course, bears any responsibility for or necessarily endorses the content of the book.

Stansfield Turner

INTRODUCTION

On THE MORNING OF February 26, 1993, a yellow Ford Econoline van parked on the second level of the public garage underneath the World Trade Center in New York City's lower Manhattan. At 12:18 P.M. there was a horrendous explosion that ripped through the garage and into the office buildings, killing six people and injuring more than 1,000. The twin towers, each 110 stories high, were shaken from their foundations to their tops, filled with smoke and without electricity. There was a crater about 120 feet in diameter and five stories deep where the bomb, estimated to be more than 1,000 pounds of high explosive, had detonated. The damage to the buildings was repaired sufficiently within twenty days for them to be reoccupied—but not so the damage to our American psyche of becoming aware that we are vulnerable to indiscriminate, unclaimed acts of terrorism.

Inevitably, there was speculation as to the consequences had it been a nuclear bomb. The A-bomb that the United States dropped on Hiroshima in August 1945 would have fit inside the Econoline van; and if one of the so-called rogue states—North Korea, Iran, Iraq, Syria, Libya, Sudan, and Afghanistan, for instance—or terrorists were to build a nuclear bomb, it would likely be a relatively simple, large, and powerful one, much like that employed at Hiroshima. That bomb released more than 10,000 times as much explosive power as the one in the van at the World Trade Center. Needless to say, had such a nuclear bomb been successfully placed and detonated in that building's garage, it would have meant terrifying consequences. Within a fraction of a second of the explosion, intense light from hot, expanding gases could set fires in buildings up to a mile away. Depending on the bomb's location inside the garage, its detonation would vaporize or destroy major foundation supports of either one or both of

1

the towers. This would, within seconds, cause one or both of the massive buildings to slowly begin to topple. Everyone within a toppled tower probably would be killed. Within seconds of detonation, chunks of building debris carrying radioactive material from the bomb would shower surrounding streets thousands of feet away. In the next minutes and hours, smaller radioactive particles would be carried by the prevailing winds and fall to the ground, creating a highly lethal radioactive area of perhaps one-half to three-quarters of a mile in width and several miles in length downwind. Some fire fighters and emergency workers inside these areas, along with citizens, would die from radiation exposure as they fought fires or tried to come to the aid of the injured. The possibility of hundreds of thousands of deaths and injuries could not be ruled out.

Even more alarming is the thought that a rogue state or terrorist group would be able to steal or purchase a nuclear warhead from a Russian weapon. It, too, would fit inside a van, and experts estimate that with some borrowed or hired expertise, it could be rigged to detonate. It would be twenty times more powerful than the Hiroshima bomb and would cause much higher levels of death and destruction, casting an unimaginable pall over our society.

These gruesome possibilities are not likely scenarios today, and neither one of them need become so *if* we face up to the challenge of preventing rogue states, terrorists, and other irresponsible actors from acquiring and employing nuclear weapons. Although the United States is working diligently on this, we are overlooking the fact that we must first reshape the U.S.-Russian nuclear relationship. However, that does not seem to be very important at a time when the possibility for nuclear war between the former adversaries has lessened so remarkably; but unless we and the Russians place our own nuclear houses in order, we will not obtain the international cooperation needed to prevent nuclear materials and technologies from falling into the hands of irresponsible nations and terrorists. We and the Russians, unfortunately, are not well positioned to elicit that cooperation because each of us still possesses more than 10,000 nuclear warheads, many more than can be justified. We are also seen by many nations without nuclear weapons to be hypocritical about wanting to reduce that number. To begin with, our current agreed-upon target of 3,500 warheads (even the next tentative level of 2,000) is still far above what we need; and our plans for getting to those numbers will take more than a decade to fulfill. Yet there is more: When all is said and done, our official policy is to employ loopholes in current agreements that permit us to maintain more than 10,000 nuclear warheads indefinitely. Ten thousand detonations like the one at Hiroshima is unimaginable; yet two-thirds of the warheads we plan to keep are much more powerful. Thus, would-be proliferators must conclude that if we see such value in possessing these weapons, they could well have equally legitimate reasons for possessing some also. We are not in a position to tell them otherwise.

Time is of the essence in correcting this situation. Every year that goes by increases the risk that rogues and terrorists will achieve their nuclear ambitions. We now know firsthand how far Iraq had progressed toward nuclear capability before it was interrupted by its defeat in the Gulf War of 1991. We know from intelligence reports that North Korea was on the brink of nuclear capability when we convinced it to stop its program, at least temporarily, in 1994. We were fortunate to be able to arrest these two attempts at proliferation, and we cannot risk letting other rogues or terrorists get that close.

This, then, is the moment for the president of the United States and congressional leaders—Republicans and Democrats alike—to step forward: If only they could break with the routines of the Cold War, they could easily accelerate the nuclear arms reduction process. Concurrently, they could help design and build an international regime to forestall any use of nuclear weapons. This book is dedicated to these momentous goals and suggests ways to move toward them without risking our nation's security. Indeed, it is difficult to conceive of a more lasting mark or more meaningful service to humankind than to seize this opportunity to eliminate once and for all time the global nuclear threat, which today has become the most important dividend of the end of the Cold War.

Part One

The Problem

1

THE SPELL CAST BY NUCLEAR WEAPONS

ONE AFTER ANOTHER THE JETS ROARED off the catapult and down the aircraft carrier's deck to be hurtled into the night sky. With only a few shielded lights about the ship, the sudden, bright-white glow of the afterburners as the pilots pushed throttles to maximum was an eerie sight. It was also an impressive scene of precision teamwork with lives constantly at stake.

I had witnessed carrier operations many times before, though my naval career had been in surface ships, not aviation. On this evening in September 1970, the flight operations had special meaning for me. I had just been promoted to rear admiral and had taken command of Task Group 60.2, the Navy's striking punch in the eastern Mediterranean Sea centered in this carrier, *USS Independence.* As I watched those aircraft taking off, I pondered my responsibilities for them. What would their specific missions be if war came? The next day I set out to find out.

I decided to start at the upper end of the Task Group's responsibilities— the possibility of nuclear war. I asked that a pilot with a nuclear mission and his bombardier brief me on what they were assigned to do if we were ordered to execute the nuclear war plan. A tall, strapping lieutenant in his late twenties and a handsome lieutenant (junior grade) a few years younger came through the door of my cabin, one carrying a targeting folder.

They began by explaining that their mission was but one of thousands in the Single Integrated Operational Plan (SIOP) for nuclear war. The

SIOP included what not only our aircraft in *Independence* would do but also the Air Force's intercontinental ballistic missiles (ICBMs) and bombers, as well as the Navy's submarine-launched ballistic missiles (SLBMs) and aircraft from other carriers. The reason for having a SIOP, they noted, was to ensure that someone attacked every target the president selected and that the attacks did not interfere with one another. The pilot then went over the flight procedures he would use to protect his aircraft from the blinding flash and immense blast effects of the very detonation he and his bombardier were going to trigger. Impatiently, I asked, "But what are you going to attack?" Their target, the lieutenant said, was a railroad bridge spanning a river in Bulgaria. Bulgaria!

I found it incredible that anyone would believe any target in Bulgaria could be more than a tertiary concern if a nuclear war was raging across Europe. Yet here were two young men prepared to risk their lives to drop a nuclear bomb on this bridge. They had their assignment and had to take it seriously. For my part, I had expected their target to be in the southern underbelly of the Soviet Union, perhaps the naval and bomber bases in the Crimea that were within range. It appeared to me this aircraft carrier had been assigned inconsequential targets because the United States had many more nuclear weapons than it needed.

For the sake of the flyers, I did my best to appear only modestly surprised. In feigning interest, I asked to look at the photograph of the bridge in the target folder they had brought along. The officers, looking a bit chagrined, pointed out that in the photo you could see where the railroad tracks stopped on either side of the river. The bridge, though, was too small to be visible! The aim point they had selected was the blank space in the river between the ends of the tracks.

About a year after this first exploration into nuclear targeting, I was on duty in the Pentagon. One of my responsibilities as chief of systems analysis for the Navy included analyzing the numbers and kinds of nuclear forces it required. One day I received an invitation to a briefing by the Air Force on the SIOP. I jumped at it. Nuclear war plans were normally shared with only a small group of officers who were more directly involved than I in nuclear matters. I hoped the briefing would shed some light on why we were bothering with a Bulgarian bridge.

On the appointed day, about fifty people gathered in a briefing room. The briefing officer had maps and charts that divided up the SIOP into several categories. He discussed whether the weapons assigned were ballistic missiles or aircraft bombs and whether they would be delivered by the Air Force or the Navy. As he went along it became clear that almost all of the targets he enumerated were military ones. Only at the very end did he discuss industrial and economic targets and the weapons allocated to them. Then I understood why so many of us had been invited to this briefing: We were being asked to persuade our superiors to support the acquisition of additional warheads in order to have enough to deal with the industrial targets more comprehensively. I asked what our inventory of nuclear warheads was at that time. The answer was about 27,000: About 20 percent were intercontinental-range strategic warheads; about 80 percent were short-range tactical warheads. The 27,000 total, however, was down from about 32,500 in 1967. The argument was that we needed to go back up.

When I went to bed that evening, I had difficulty getting to sleep. I kept thinking, "That was the most frightening briefing I've ever heard."

These two incidents—the review of the SIOP I had received onboard ship and the Pentagon briefing on it—were the first seeds for this book.

COMMON SENSE TELLS US that 27,000 nuclear warheads, let alone the peak of 32,500, far exceeded any conceivable need the United States could possibly have had. How unrealistic were such numbers? It would take 55 billion aircraft bombs, each bomb containing 500 pounds of TNT, to unleash as much energy as 32,500 nuclear warheads.[1] To put this in perspective, each state in the union could be carpeted with 1 billion bombs with 5 billion to spare—something quite beyond imagination. To put it another way: The power of the 32,500 warheads would roughly equal 1 million Hiroshima-type bombs,[2] one of which destroyed almost all of the buildings within a 12-square-mile area and killed 140,000 of the city's 350,000 people during the first five months after detonation.[3]

Of our maximum of 32,500 warheads, some were for intercontinental-range weapons to attack industrial or population targets or to destroy installations that were hardened against nuclear attack. Others were small (by nuclear standards; they were enormous by those of conventional weapons) and for short-range use on the battlefield. There have to be plans for utilizing each category, and those plans can be complex (e.g., if a large warhead arrived within about twenty minutes of an earlier one, the second might be neutralized by the debris thrown up by the first). With such large numbers of warheads and the variety of options for employing them, by the 1980s our nuclear war plan filled more than one million pages. General Lee Butler told me that when he took over command of the Strategic Air Command (SAC) in 1991 (in 1992 SAC became the Strategic Command [StratCom], which Butler commanded until 1994), he began a month-long effort to review every aspect of the master war plan, including each of the 12,000-plus targets. One of his conclusions was that no single person on his staff had a grasp of all of the factors essential to creating a coherent nuclear war plan. Such complexity in nuclear war plans makes it almost impossible for anyone to be certain that directives from the president or the secretary of defense are actually reflected in them. Some experts have even asserted that declaratory policy changes by presidents and secretaries have often resulted in few, if any, changes to the plans themselves. And given this million-page complexity, it has been difficult for presidents to appreciate fully what options they had or to be ready to inject new ones of their own during a crisis. Rather small changes could have such interlocking effects that it could take a year to insert them. For much of the nuclear era, presidents were effectively limited to a small number of options—all involving massive numbers of weapons.

It is almost incomprehensible that there was so little questioning of the merit of adding or subtracting warheads from the base of tens of thousands. How could anyone have been so concerned about the difference between 27,000 and 32,500 as to warrant the lobbying effort to which I had been subjected? It was not until the late 1980s that anyone in high authority addressed the issue of excess of targets in our war plans head-on. Why did it take so long to do this? In part, intense secrecy made it difficult for decisionmakers to know just what was going on. Yet there have been thousands of officials in the executive branch and in Congress who were privy to an annual directive signed by the president specifying the number of nuclear warheads we would have for the next year. It should have been easy enough to recognize that 32,500 warheads was an unconscionably high number, regardless of the number that the Soviets, and later the Russians, possessed. In my view it was just too difficult for those officials to tear themselves away from the logic of conventional warfare, where it is always better to have more weapons than your opponent. And because the stakes seemed so high, the military planners grossly overestimated the allowance needed for possible faulty weapons, approximating two warheads for every target requiring one. And finally, from a psychological and emotional perspective, it seemed essential to national security planners that we stay ahead in the race for "superiority" as well as espouse the view that we could "win" even in a nuclear war. President Ronald Reagan's first secretary of defense, Caspar Weinberger, stated it clearly: "You show me a secretary of defense who is planning not to prevail [in nuclear war], and I'll show you a secretary of defense who ought to be impeached."[4] This hyperbole reflected the fact that any political leader who did not think we should spend enough to win in nuclear war ran the danger of being called soft on communism. One analyst of this situation noted that "no administration has been able to disavow the prospect of emerging from a nuclear conflict with some kind of meaningful victory."[5]

What we did, then, was to make parity with the Soviets our minimum level of comfort. Accordingly, we kept ratcheting our number of weapons upward as they did theirs, in their own quest for at least parity. This situation was compounded by the fact that our stated objective has always been deterrence. Deterrence requires posing a threat of unacceptable damage in retaliation to any attack with nuclear weapons. As the opponent's nuclear arsenal increased, we felt ours had to also, lest our deterrent threat somehow diminish. Deterrence, however, is in the eye of the beholder. We just never asked whether the Soviets, if they had more nuclear capability than we, would really feel that we could no longer pose a threat of unacceptable retaliation.

The more nuclear weapons we had, the greater the risks we took in managing them. In contriving uses for nuclear weapons in war plans, planners came closer and closer to intellectual dishonesty. This way of thinking was set at the very beginning, when President Harry Truman directed that the first atom bomb be employed against a military target. The Army Air Corps selected a military headquarters in Hiroshima. It may well have been an important military target, but it was also at the center of the city. Most of the 70,000 people who died immediately, and the additional 70,000 who died within the next few months, were not associated with that headquarters. It is easy to believe that the people who selected the target were hypocritical in pretending it was a military target, since most of the bomb's impact would be against nonmilitary targets. And

though that must have been very clear to them, these planners were required to select a target that when destroyed would stun the Japanese into
surrender. Whatever their motives or consciences, those first nuclear targeteers were forced to face up to *the* moral dilemma of the nuclear era:
how to take advantage of the vast power of these weapons without unwanted ancillary effects.

We had been quietly avoiding this dilemma with the firebombings of
Dresden, Tokyo, and five other Japanese cities during the final six months
of World War II.* After Hiroshima we could not avoid it. The further we
have moved from World War II, the more public deference we have paid
to morality in nuclear targeting. For more than thirty years our declaratory policy has been that we do not target cities. That, however, has not by
any means solved matters. For instance, in the 1980s one of our war plans,
which supposedly did not target cities, included fifteen nuclear detonations within ten miles of the Kremlin. Again, if this was not hypocrisy, it
was an example of targeteers being caught between conflicting requirements: one to accomplish sufficient damage, the other to avoid cities. Because it fell to military planners to somehow resolve such antithetical demands, they have shaped our nuclear strategy—to the point where one
must question whether the system has always been under adequate civilian control.

Dissembling in nuclear planning, though, has not been a matter for
military planners alone. It reached to the highest levels of government in
our doctrine to help defend West European allies. This began in 1952 at a
meeting of NATO's foreign ministers in Lisbon. NATO's military planners
had assessed the Warsaw Pact's conventional military capabilities as being
considerably superior to those of NATO, and so a goal was developed to
field a total of ninety-six army divisions and associated forces, up from
fewer than forty, many of which were skeletal. This was politically unacceptable to Europeans, as it appeared to set the stage for yet another large
conventional war in Europe; it was economically unacceptable on both
sides of the Atlantic. Instead, NATO ministers accepted the nuclear superiority of the United States over the Soviet Union as establishing a general

---

*In total, our firebombings of Japanese cities killed more people than were killed immediately at
both Hiroshima and Nagasaki. The directives to the targeting people in those cases, however, were for
attacks on the cities themselves. There was no pretense at aiming at a military target. Hence, there was
no issue of hypocrisy for the planners.

equilibrium. This was not a difficult concept for the United States to accept at the time, since there was relatively little risk. The Soviets had detonated their first nuclear device only three years before, built less than ten
nuclear warheads compared with our approximately 450, and possessed
very little potential for delivering warheads at intercontinental distances.
Soviet nuclear capabilities grew over the next decade, however, offsetting
our advantage to some extent. As Europeans looked for additional reas-
surance, it could only come from our being more specific as to just how
our nuclear superiority would translate into the defense of Europe.

At a meeting of NATO's foreign and defense ministers in Athens in
1962, U.S. Secretary of Defense Robert S. McNamara suggested the possibility of halting "a Soviet advance into Western Europe by unilateral ap-
plication of nuclear weapons on or near the battlefield."[6] This eased us
into a pledge to initiate the use of nuclear weapons if necessary to repulse
an invasion of Western Europe, even one by conventional forces of the
Warsaw Pact. In 1967, NATO formally adopted nuclear response to conventional attack as its doctrine. For years, we assumed that disrupting the
Warsaw Pact's rear echelons in Eastern Europe with tactical nuclear attacks would halt an advance: What we failed to address was whether the
Soviets would respond in kind against NATO forces in Western Europe.

By the late 1960s, the Soviets had sufficient nuclear capabilities to do
that. For Europe, with its limited geographical size, this could mean the
loss of much of what was being defended. The Europeans sidestepped this
dilemma by hypothesizing an American nuclear umbrella over all of Europe. If a conventional war being waged inside that umbrella went badly,
they presumed the Americans would launch attacks with long-range nuclear weapons directly on the Soviet Union and outside the umbrella.
That, of course, would open the United States to nuclear retaliation.
Americans, in contrast, assumed we would employ short-range tactical
nuclear weapons inside the umbrella, and we made our intentions obvious by deploying some 7,000 of them to Europe. In 1979 Henry Kissinger
pointed out, albeit after leaving the government, the unreasonableness of
what the Europeans were expecting from us: "The European allies should
not keep asking us to multiply strategic assurances that we cannot possibly mean, or if we do mean, we should not want to execute, because if we
execute we risk the destruction of civilization."[7] Despite these irreconcil-
able positions, we and the Europeans continue to profess that under a

policy of "extended deterrence" the United States will employ nuclear weapons to defend its allies against attacks by conventional forces, not just nuclear ones.

This bluff may well have contributed to deterring the Soviets from invading Western Europe. It certainly saved us and our allies the considerable costs of maintaining larger conventional forces to do the same. But this begs the question: Should we have placed the survival of Western Europe on the line in order to get those savings? It was not just an abstract risk we were taking. U.S. military forces in Europe were poised to use nuclear weapons the moment the fighting went against them (otherwise those weapons might be overrun, and without them we might lose the war). General Bernard W. Rogers, the Supreme Allied Commander in Europe, said in 1984, "Because of our lack of sustainability—primarily ammunition, materials to replace losses on the battlefield, tanks, howitzers, trained manpower . . . I have to request the release of nuclear weapons fairly quickly after a conventional attack. And I'm talking in terms of days, not in terms of weeks or months."[8] The risk is that a military organization trained on a set of assumptions is all too prone to work from those assumptions in the event of a crisis.

But there is an even more hair-raising risk that we have taken and are continuing to take: the obsession with surprise nuclear attack. There is a thesis that assumes the Soviets (and even the Russians today) might try to disable our retaliatory capability through one swift blow and thus "win" a nuclear war. A 1954 study of the vulnerability of SAC bases, conducted by RAND, a corporation formed and funded by the U.S. Air Force in early 1946 to do analytic work on military problems, concluded the Soviets could wipe out our entire SAC bomber force with a few dozen bombers in a surprise attack. It argued that the mere possession of nuclear weapons and delivery capability was not sufficient to deter such attack. If we were to really deter a surprise attack, the Soviets had to be persuaded that our strategic forces could survive an attack and then surmount any barriers to retaliation (such as defenses or civil defense preparations) to deliver a crushing retaliatory blow. As it developed over time, this view held that any adverse changes in the balance of strategic forces or sudden technological breakthroughs—perhaps in antimissile defenses or antisubmarine warfare—could upset a stable balance by creating what came to be known as a "window of vulnerability" to a surprise attack. Hence, no set number of nuclear forces could assure stable deterrence; rather, we always had to stay ahead of the Soviets quantitatively and qualitatively. Later, other worst case scenarios were added, including a sneak attack to destroy our command and control capability and a "decapitating attack" on our political leadership. All this was applying the deeply ingrained lessons of Pearl Harbor to the nuclear era erroneously because:

- The estimates of Soviet strength, technology, and force readiness were inflated. A major point here is that the strategists at RAND, up to mid-1961, had to rely on wildly inflated Air Force intelligence estimates. They did not have access to the super-sensitive intelligence sources. These included the U-2 and RB-70 spy planes, photographic reconnaissance satellites, signal intercepts, and agents on the ground. From 1961 on, these sources confirmed that the United States had never trailed in technology or numbers of strategic launch vehicles, and that the United States, at worst, would have had several hours' warning as to secret Soviet preparations for a surprise attack (and more likely several days or weeks).
- The Soviets would have great difficulty executing a complicated simultaneous strategic strike at far-flung targets without giving us warning enough to retaliate. And after the first strategic ballistic missile submarine (SSBN) came on line in 1960, it became impossible for the Soviets to destroy all of our retaliatory capacity in a surprise attack.
- The Soviet Union, having lost 20 million people in World War II, would hardly be indifferent to a death toll of equal magnitude in a nuclear exchange.
- The Soviets would pay an enormous price if a surprise attack failed.

Nonetheless, we took substantial risks to ward off surprise attacks on our ICBMs and bombers by creating an elaborate warning system that enables us to launch a response between the time we detect an incoming attack and the time it actually impacts. The flight time of a ballistic missile from Russia to the United States is twenty-five to thirty minutes. Within two to seven minutes of launch we should have detected and identified

TABLE 1.1   Best and Worst Cases for Firing Our ICBMs Under Attack from Russia

				Time of Impact
	0 2	12	20	30
Best Case	Time to Detect Attack	Time to Assemble Principals	Time to Decide	Time to Relay Orders and Fire Own Missiles

				Time of Impact
	0 7 10			25
Worst Case	Time to Detect Attack	Time to Assemble Principals and Decide	Time to Relay Orders and Fire Own Missiles	

any massive attack. There are elaborate procedures for cross-checking and evaluating the evidence while gathering senior military commanders and civilian officials on a conference telephone call. That could mean rousing people out of a sound sleep, interrupting meetings, locating those who are playing golf or shopping, and so on. There would be duty officers continuously in the command centers of the major military commands, the Pentagon, and the White House, but the probability of getting most of the principal officials whom the president knows and trusts (e.g., the secretary of defense) on the phone within five to ten minutes is not high. Once these officials assembled, they would need some time to ask their own questions and to make their own evaluations before deciding to bring in the president. Scrambling a president summarily is not something that can be done cavalierly, especially if the commander in chief is engaged in some very public activity.

Yet the president would be facing a very short deadline once brought into the debate. At least ten minutes, and more likely fifteen, would be needed to transmit an order to launch our weapons, to verify it, and to give the missiles and bombers time enough to launch and fly far enough away to avoid the effects of the incoming attack. That means there could be as little as three minutes to assemble principals and for the president to decide and at the very most eighteen minutes for making the most momentous decision in history. It is irresponsible even to pretend we have the capability for making a decision of this import under these conditions—or that we would do so even if we could.

However, maintaining the pretense of being able to launch on warning has been an additional way of dissuading the Soviets and now the Russians from attempting a surprise attack. Yet that benefit must be weighed against the risk of keeping a large part of our nuclear force on constant hair-trigger alert. We have had thousands of false alarms of impending missile attacks on the United States, and a few could have spun out of control. One such incident took place on June 3, 1980. Zbigniew "Zbig" Brzezinski, President Carter's assistant for national security affairs, was awakened at 2:26 A.M. by a phone call from Colonel William Odom, a staff officer responsible for matters of nuclear readiness. Odom told him the warning system was predicting a nuclear attack of 220 missiles on the United States with the specific destination unknown. The alarm bells of nuclear alert were ringing, and the conference calls were under way. Shortly thereafter, Odom called back to say the warning indicators had changed to an all-out attack of 2,220 missiles. Bomber crews on alert were manning their aircraft and the Pacific Command's airborne command post had taken off. What flashed through Brzezinski's mind was that in less than thirty minutes it would be all over for him and most other Washingtonians. He was determined to ensure that the Soviet Union would be equally devastated but decided he had another minute before having to wake President Carter and confront him with a decision on whether to launch a counterattack immediately. He asked Odom to give him one more update. Odom called again almost immediately to say that only one of our warning stations had reported the impending attack. The fact that no other station saw it indicated there was a computer error in the system. The crisis came and went in a matter of minutes.[9]

Still, the chances of our going to war on the basis of a false alarm have always been low. A president would see that releasing any nuclear weapons under such a circumstance would virtually guarantee that the United States would be subjected to a nuclear strike, if indeed one had not already been launched. The president would also understand it would be foolhardy to place anything like 100 percent confidence in any intelligence report about an impending attack. The consequences of being wrong could be so enormous that, I believe, any president would wait it out rather than make nuclear war certain.

Nuclear theorists think up and organize these elaborate procedures for firing nuclear weapons under pressure and for initiating nuclear war in the defense of allies. Since Nagasaki, there is no evidence that a president would have likely released nuclear weapons without an actual nuclear provocation. In short, there is a world of difference between concocting theories for the use of nuclear weapons and shouldering the responsibility of actually employing them. What would happen, though, if the system slipped from the president's control as a result of an accident or confusion during a crisis? If it fell into the hands of people we have trained in these theories, would they follow their training or be restrained by the weight of their decision? There is no way to know, but it is a sobering and dangerous aspect of our military posture, even today.

Another chilling aspect of that posture has been the physical dangers to which we have subjected the American people and others. The most glaring case was in 1961 when one of our B-52 strategic bombers broke up in flight over North Carolina. Two nuclear bombs of megaton size landed near Greensboro. On one, five of the six safety switches failed. Only the last prevented detonation. Fortunately, the only untoward result was that some radioactive materials were spread over a small area.[10] This incident was one of eleven in which nuclear weapons were accidentally lost from aircraft in flight or were involved in accidents in aircraft during the 1960s, when we maintained strategic bombers on continuous airborne alert. We also have had accidents involving U.S. submarines with nuclear weapons embarked, none with any nuclear detonations.

The end of the Cold War has lulled us into believing we no longer need be concerned about the kinds of excesses and risks we have seen with respect to nuclear weapons. We no longer feel that a nuclear defense of Europe is necessary or that a surprise nuclear attack from Russia is at all likely. And we do not feel that a major nuclear confrontation, such as that experienced during the 1962 Cuban missile crisis, is likely. There are reasons, however, why such attitudes could prove to be negligently short-sighted.

First, we must recognize that there are a lot of nuclear weapons around. The bulk are in the United States, with more than 15,000, and Russia, with more than 20,000. China has about 500, France and Great Britain something less than that.[11] In addition, there are three "nuclear threshold" states—Israel, Pakistan, and India, none of which acknowledges being a nuclear power. The general assumption is that Israel has 100-plus weapons immediately available and that Pakistan and India have the capability of assembling modest numbers of nuclear weapons quite rapidly.

Second, there is the overarching concern that since nuclear weapons are likely to be with us indefinitely, the existence of our society in anything like its present form will be at risk as far ahead as we can see. With consequences of that magnitude, we must remain positively engaged, no matter how slim we judge the probability of nuclear catastrophe to be. It is as basic as a homeowner's taking out insurance against the small chance the house will burn down. Even if all nuclear weapons were somehow to be destroyed, preventing the manufacture of new ones would require diligent attention. After all, the knowledge of how to make them cannot be erased. In short, we have a vitally important responsibility to future generations.

Third, we cannot predict where Russia will be in even a few years. It does not seem likely that its economic base will permit Russia to be a confrontational adversary again for a decade or more. Unfortunately, that does not mean nuclear tensions could not regenerate. Today's Russian leaders are saying they cannot afford sufficient conventional forces to match those of NATO and therefore must rely more on nuclear military power—the same tack we took in offering a nuclear umbrella to our NATO allies during the Cold War. Ultimately, Russia will again be a great power, and we do not want our nuclear relationship to return to being a tense one. We should do all we can to make that unlikely while we have the opportunity.

Fourth, whereas during the Cold War our dominant concern in the nuclear arena was a major nuclear war with the Soviet Union, we must now include a wider range of contingencies:

- There is the possibility that nuclear weapons will proliferate to rogue states and terrorists and that they will employ them deliberately.
- There is the risk of accidental, unauthorized, and mistaken use by the nuclear states. Today, the five declared nuclear powers (the

United States, Russia, China, Great Britain, and France) as well as
the three threshold states (Israel, India, and Pakistan) have all
shown considerable caution in controlling their nuclear
capabilities. Still, the risk of accident or error exists and would be
much greater if a state like Iraq or North Korea was able to
procure a small nuclear arsenal because emphasis on secrecy could
conflict with establishing firm internal controls.
- Finally, there is the possibility of deliberate, rational use of nuclear
weapons by existing nuclear powers and threshold states. An
Indian-Pakistani nuclear war could erupt; Israel could believe
itself sufficiently endangered to resort to a nuclear defense; Russia
could feel threatened by China, or feel it is unable to meet
problems with neighbors with conventional force; and China is a
great uncertainty when we look to the future, although its current
policy is no first-use.

Thus, with the end of the Cold War we must widen the focus of our efforts to deter nuclear catastrophe. Russia still remains the threat of greatest magnitude and, therefore, must remain our primary concern. Lesser
threats from lesser nuclear powers are more likely to occur. If we look
ahead a quarter- or half-century, as we surely must in this analysis, it is
not beyond imagination that world affairs could degenerate into occa-
sional, limited use of nuclear weapons and even some deliberate, accidental, and unauthorized employment of them. That would be a vastly different world in which to live, what with uninhabitable, pockmarked areas of
contamination and the constant threat of instant, indiscriminate destruction hanging over populations. This is not necessarily the most likely nuclear direction, but it is a grim prospect. Our policies on nuclear weapons
must deal with Russia as well as all the other nuclear powers. In deciding
how we deal with each, it should be evident that it would be a mere coin-
cidence if the policies formulated in the crucible of the Cold War happened to be those best suited for the new world.

Most of our efforts during the Cold War to prevent the use of nuclear
weapons—bilateral agreements between the United States and the Soviet
Union, for the most part—have been of limited value thus far. The latest
treaty, START II, promises to reduce intercontinental strategic nuclear
warheads actually mated to delivery vehicles to 3,000–3,500 on each side

(roughly one-third of what we possessed at the end of the Cold War) by 2003. That helps by establishing that both major nuclear powers want a future with far fewer nuclear weapons, but 3,000–3,500 warheads would still constitute a grim threat to both societies. There is, then, no reason to worry less because of this numerically impressive achievement. Moreover, the numbers are misleading. They do not include tactical nuclear warheads for short-range weapons and strategic warheads held in reserve and not mated to long-range delivery vehicles. Add these, and the United States intends to maintain more than 10,000 warheads; the Russian figure is uncertain but could well be larger. At these levels each side could do so much damage that the reduction would be rendered meaningless: What does it matter whether we incinerate one another with 10,000 warheads or with 32,500?

There are other bilateral arms control agreements for which we have congratulated ourselves. Several limit the size of ballistic missiles and the number of warheads they carry. We have wanted to limit the number of Soviet warheads because of their supposed value in conducting a surprise attack. But we have such an overwhelming, assured capability to retaliate after a preemptive strike that this sort of limit is of minor import to deterring surprise attacks. Other steps we and the Russians have taken—without written agreement—are to remove some nuclear weapons from conditions of high alert and to shift the immediate targeting coordinates of others to spots in the oceans. These are commendable moves symbolically but purely cosmetic. For instance, Russian missiles do have their target set on "zero" but can be reset in ten seconds; and if a missile were launched accidentally or illicitly, it would automatically switch back to its primary wartime target.[12]

Our second major approach to controlling nuclear weapons has been to pressure, cajole, and legally tie the hands of would-be proliferators and those abetting them—and we have been eminently successful here. South Africa voluntarily disposed of its five or six nuclear weapons; Ukraine, Belarus, and Kazakhstan returned to Russia all of the Soviet weapons that were in their territories when the USSR dissolved; we forestalled Iraqi and North Korean programs to develop nuclear weapons, at least for the time being (it remains unclear whether North Korea produced any weapons previously).

Still, the know-how for manufacturing nuclear weapons is openly available; more and more fissionable material is accumulating and generating

a black market; Russian control over fissionable materials, nuclear technology, and even weapons themselves is increasingly seen as inadequate;
and more countries are acquiring the sophisticated skills needed for manufacturing nuclear weapons as part of competing in the world market-
place. Yet assembling the materials and skills and actually manufacturing
a nuclear weapon is not something that can be done in a garage by any
mechanic. On balance, however, rogue states would likely be satisfied with
a large, crude, Hiroshima-type nuclear weapon with fewer tolerances; terrorists might even be content with nonexplosive, radioactive-contaminat-
ing devices. We would be naive to assume that if rogue states and terrorist
groups have reason to believe acquiring nuclear weapons would be to
their advantage, they will not do so.

The incentives these parties see for proliferation today are: to gain
leverage over traditional enemies; to deter a traditional enemy that has acquired them; to deter the United States from intervening with its superior
conventional forces; and to terrorize the United States from spreading
democracy and free enterprise around the world. Those incentives will
persist as long as there is a perception that nuclear weapons can be employed usefully for such purposes. The United States is perpetuating that
very perception by claiming it needs nuclear weapons to defend its allies
against conventional military assaults. This undermines one of our major
efforts against proliferation: the Nuclear Non-Proliferation Treaty
(NPT),* which originally dates to 1968 and was renewed indefinitely in
1995 by 178 nations. Other nations can legitimately argue that they have
similar vital interests that justify their acquiring nuclear weapons, even if
it means abrogating the NPT. And they have an additional excuse in a
provision of the NPT that requires the existing nuclear powers to do all
they can to reduce the size of their nuclear arsenals with the objective of
total elimination. If START II is fully implemented in 2003, we and the
Russians will only be down to approximately the number of warheads we
had at the time the NPT was signed; it is difficult to deny that progress on

---

*Under the NPT, the five declared nuclear states (Britain, China, France, Russia, and the United
States) agree not to proliferate nuclear weapons, to share benefits of peaceful nuclear technology with
nonweapon states that are NPT parties, and to pursue "in good faith" negotiations to end the arms
race and achieve general and complete disarmament. The nonweapon states agree not to acquire nuclear weapons or nuclear explosive devices and to submit their peaceful nuclear facilities and materials to International Atomic Energy Agency (IAEA) safeguards.

that front has been slow. The NPT, then, will be less of an assurance than we would like to believe until we and the Russians renounce claims that we have needs for these weapons and make much greater reductions.

The Comprehensive Test Ban Treaty (CTBT), which bans any testing of nuclear weapons, is another achievement more of form than substance. It is supposed to be a barrier to proliferation, but Israel, Pakistan, and South Africa all developed their weapons without detectable testing (as did the United States with the weapon dropped on Hiroshima). Testing primarily provides confidence that a new, highly complex weapon will work. For rogue states and terrorists, moderate confidence in rather simple weapons that have not been tested will suffice. We would do well not to count too heavily on the CTBT to inhibit proliferation. And once a state breaks through the barriers to proliferation, there could be a snowball effect. For instance, should Iraq acquire these weapons, Iran would scramble to match its arch rival, and Saudi Arabia could feel exposed and want to follow suit. This is what happened in India, which acquired nuclear capability because it felt vulnerable to China's nuclear weapons; Pakistan then believed it had to match its neighbor. Should there be much additional proliferation, even responsible nations like Germany and Japan would feel pressure to develop their own nuclear weapons.

Pointing out that there are limits to what arms control agreements have achieved is not to belittle them. These are major accomplishments, done with great skill and patience and under difficult circumstances. Their value, however, has been less in specific actions than in committing the two major nuclear powers to lower numbers and to more rigorous controls. Unfortunately, the outlook for using the arms control process to make further progress in these directions is not good. The more difficult challenges lie ahead: going to low numbers of weapons—where concern with cheating will be considerable—and expanding negotiations to include all other nuclear powers. The best evidence of this is the agreements on arms control made by Presidents Clinton and Yeltsin at their March 1997 summit. In their efforts just to sustain momentum, they found it necessary to slow the arms control process, to complicate it, and to push difficult issues down the road. Specifically, they postponed full implementation of START II by five years; forced a second ratification of the revised START II by the U.S. Senate; and limited their ambition for a START III to 2,000–2,500 warheads each and not until the end of 2010. What this tells us is that an already glacially slow process is confronting such problems that it is moving slower—and that we have no plan for getting across a threshold low enough to reduce meaningfully the nuclear threat under which we live.

Overcoming these impediments should be a topic of concern for every citizen. Even though most of us assume the problems of nuclear weapons are a secondary concern today, the amount of media coverage the issue receives shows a continuing interest in our nuclear future. Several surveys of articles in the *New York Times* and the *Washington Post* taken at random during 1996 revealed one or two articles per day in each paper touching on one or more of the following topics: nuclear proliferation; the outlook for various treaties governing these weapons; intelligence on nuclear weapons; nuclear terrorism; ballistic missile defenses; future requirements for numbers and types of nuclear weapons and their delivery systems; the contaminating aftereffects of past nuclear programs.[13]

Yet despite such evidence of national concern, there is strong resistance to changing our Cold War nuclear policies. A full-scale Nuclear Posture Review (NPR) was conducted by the Pentagon in 1994. It concluded that our current policies and programs were just about right, except that we should use the looseness of START II to maintain the 10,000 warheads in inventory noted earlier, rather than the 3,000–3,500 permitted to be mated to operational strategic delivery vehicles. Similarly, when the U.S. Senate ratified START II in 1996, it admonished the president to regulate the process of reductions so that the number of warheads possessed by Russia in no case would exceed the number possessed by the United States to the extent that a strategic imbalance could endanger our security.

It is easy to explain this resistance to changing U.S. nuclear weapons policies. One important reason is persistent habits left over from the Cold War—like besting the Soviets in every conceivable category. The rivalry between the U.S. Air Force and the U.S. Navy to maintain their respective shares of nuclear forces also came into play at times. There is also the military's tradition of always wanting to have more weapons than one's opponent. Perhaps the ultimate cause, however, is that we have been mesmerized by having tapped the most fundamental source of power, that which binds atoms together. For the past fifty years we have been fixated on the conclusion that such power can somehow be put to use.

Part Two

The Theory

2

POINTS OF NON-RECOVERY

As Director of Central Intelligence,[1] I was required to brief the Committee on the Armed Services of the House of Representatives annually on the balance of nuclear forces between the United States and the USSR. My first such briefing, in the spring of 1977, consisted of a summation of the numbers and types of nuclear weapons on each side. During the question period, a boyish-looking member from Suffolk County, New York, Tom Downey, complained that my charts, which showed how many of this type of missile the Soviets had and how many of that type we had, were not very edifying. Missiles were not just missiles, he said. One packs more punch than another—for instance, if its guidance system is more accurate. Downey even cited the formula that relates the accuracy and explosive power of a weapon to its total lethality. I didn't know the formula, but I could see his point. I was embarrassed.

I worked with the experts at CIA to devise different ways of comparing the lethal potential of the U.S. and Soviet arsenals. We started from the point that nuclear weapons have two functions: to destroy targets specially hardened against nuclear attack, like the silos in which ICBMs are housed, and to level wide areas of nonhardened structures, like cities or air bases. We compared the theoretical potential of each country in these two operational categories. The Soviets were ahead in each. What was more, they could tip that balance even further if they attacked first and caught our nuclear forces off their guard. Thus, it was not the prewar balance that would count but how much of our lethal potential would still be available after a surprise preemptive attack by the Soviets. Would there be enough retaliatory potential to pose a devastating threat? If so, that should deter them from attempting one. We looked at the worst possible case—assuming the Soviets would launch the most disabling attack they could and that we would simply ride it out. We then assessed the number of hard targets and the size of the urban area in the Soviet Union that our surviving nuclear forces would still be able to destroy. The result was revealing and meaningful: No matter what the Soviets did, and despite their being ahead of us quantitatively, the United States could still level the entire urban area of the Soviet Union between one and two times. Put simply, in the worst case imaginable we had much more than enough invulnerable retaliatory force to destroy the Soviet Union as a society. I was encouraged, because I could now tell Downey and his colleagues something relevant to the decisions they had to make.

Alas, the conclusion was all too meaningful for the Pentagon. It sent a clear message that the United States possessed more than enough nuclear weaponry. Yet at that very moment our military was proposing to build still another ICBM, the MX. The rationale was that our existing mix of forces was too vulnerable to surprise attack, something our analysis clearly disputed. The Pentagon's argument against us at CIA, that we in the intelligence field were doing war-gaming and that was not our province, was a sterile bureaucratic ploy.

As we debated this into 1980, I found myself increasingly isolated. Even the CIA's analysts were not behind me. They were concerned not to get the CIA involved in the debate over the MX. There is a strong ethic among intelligence professionals that they must not take sides on policy issues, lest they be accused of slanting the intelligence to support their views. Intelligence analyses, however, must be relevant to policymaking. This one was, and it laid out the facts without taking sides.

In December 1980, despite the objections of the secretary of defense, I sent this analysis to President Carter. It was customary to permit those who dissented with an intelligence report to include their contrary views in it. In this instance, the military intelligence organizations dissented, as did, with my permission, my own staff at CIA. It revealed to me how deeply embedded the view was that more is better. The CIA's analysts, having spent years carefully measuring whether we matched the Soviets in every category of nuclear capability, simply could not countenance being the ones to reveal that we did not need to be equal in order to deter.

NUCLEAR WEAPONS ARE NOT only much more powerful than conventional ones but also qualitatively different. It is not too far-fetched to think of them as small pieces of sun brought to earth, creating effects otherwise not experienced. That nuclear weapons are a species unto themselves is best shown by the terminology we employ to describe their power. The pound is the unit of measure for the explosive in conventional munitions. For nuclear munitions the unit of measure is the metric tonne, but the weapons are so powerful that we must measure their force in kilotons (KT—thousands of tonnes) and even megatons (MT—millions of tonnes). Five hundred pounds of TNT is the typical explosive force of a common conventional bomb; in contrast, a common warhead in Russia's strategic arsenal carries 550 KT of force. A 550-KT weapon is the equivalent of 550 × 1,000 (kilo) × 2,200 (lbs./metric tonne), that is, 1,210,000,000 pounds of conventional explosive. A freight train 150 miles long would be needed to transport that much conventional explosive to an airfield. It would take more than 25,000 sorties by our most modern bomber, the B-2, to deliver that much conventional explosive. In the course of some 44,000 aircraft sorties during the six-week air campaign in the Gulf War in 1991, we dropped only 84,000 metric tonnes of conventional bombs, or less than one-fifth of the explosive force of a single 550-KT nuclear bomb.[2]

It is understandable that we prefer to use MT and KT instead of ten-figure numerals when evaluating the force of nuclear weapons; the acronyms are much handier. Doing so, however, has encouraged us to talk rather cavalierly about the magnitude of the power involved. For instance, it is not so incongruous to talk about a "small" nuclear warhead when we label it as .1 KT. A warhead of that size fits on an artillery shell and is the equivalent of .1 × 1,000 (kilo) × 2,200 (lbs./tonne) or 220,000 pounds of conventional explosive. That means that every time a nuclear artillery shell is fired it is the same as launching five fully loaded B-2 bombers at the target.

We must, however, be careful. Equating 550 KT of nuclear explosive with 1.2 billion pounds of conventional explosive, or .1 KT of nuclear with 220,000 pounds, greatly understates the difference, because such comparisons account for only the blast effects of the two kinds of weapons and ignore four additional effects of nuclear weapons:

- An extraordinarily intense flash of light and heat can kill people and ignite fires miles from the point of detonation. These fires, which occur within milliseconds, can initiate firestorms over areas of tens to hundreds of square miles with average air temperatures well above the boiling point of water and average wind speeds of hurricane force. The high winds can overturn flammables like stoves and gasoline pumps and start additional fires. Overturned stoves are believed to have been the major source of fires at Hiroshima.[3]

- There will be enormous amounts of radioactivity. Immediate, direct radiation from a 550-KT airburst, that is, where the fireball explodes above and does not touch the ground, can kill people within several miles. When the fireball does touch the ground, radioactivity attached to particles lifted into the air by the explosion could carry, depending on wind conditions and other factors, literally around the globe and be deposited tens, hundreds, or even thousands of miles from the explosion. Because the effects of radioactivity vary widely given weather, wind, and the nature of the soil and infrastructure at ground zero, they can only be approximated. Typically, it is estimated that a 1-MT detonation near the ground at the center of Detroit would contaminate a cigar-shaped zone reaching as far as Pittsburgh, 250 miles away. Some areas within that zone would be too contaminated to inhabit for periods ranging from a few days to ten years; for example, an area about 200 miles by 100 miles would be uninhabitable for one month, an area about 100 miles by ten miles for a year. (The modest explosion at the Chernobyl nuclear power plant in the Soviet Union in 1986 deposited radioactive material some 1,500 miles away in Norway; reindeer there became so contaminated from eating the vegetation that they were not fit for human consumption.) Additionally, an area around a groundburst cannot be inhabited for years (e.g., an area of 1,200 square miles adjacent to the Chernobyl plant has been uninhabitable since the explosion, and some 30,000 square miles of farmland can be only partially cultivated).[4] Because radioactivity can carry so far, any groundburst will endanger cities, even if detonation occurs on a remote military target.

Russian ICBM silos are so hardened, for instance, that U.S. plans for destroying them at times called for employing two large, near-groundburst warheads. That would send a massive amount of radioactive particles into the atmosphere. In the Soviet Union, some ICBM silos were directly upwind of major cities, including Moscow. There are fewer Russian ICBMs so located today, but any major attack on them would still cause serious contamination problems in cities.

- An electromagnetic pulse (EMP) of thousands of volts can be expected to overload electrical circuits and disrupt or destroy power, communications, and computer networks and other critical electrical systems. A single, deliberate EMP burst high over the center of the United States would likely cause a temporary electrical and communications blackout nationwide.

- Environmental damage of several sorts is likely. Since trees and many other plants are roughly as susceptible to radiation exposure as are people, any area exposed to levels of radiation high enough to kill or injure people would be deforested or depleted of plant life. This, in turn, would have implications for soil erosion and for the survival prospects of wildlife and domesticated animals. For example, insects, which are more resistant to radiation than birds, would no longer be subject to predators. This, in turn, could lead to wild fluctuations in the size of insect populations in the new ecological system created by the elimination of predators and plant life. Numerous nuclear explosions could also create sufficient nitric oxides to deplete the ozone layer twenty to thirty kilometers above the earth. This would expose humans and animals to higher than normal ultraviolet radiation. Although the physics of ozone depletion is not fully understood, the consequences of ozone depletion could be serious. There is also the thesis of "nuclear winter," which holds that vast fires started by a large nuclear attack would cause smoke and particles in the atmosphere to cut off the sun's rays for an extended period, with a subsequent cooling effect. Although the surface temperature change might not be as severe as suggested in early analyses of the potential for nuclear winter, there are enough effects associated with nuclear winter that it cannot be discounted entirely.

All of these unique effects of nuclear weapons have been and still are either totally ignored or severely discounted in U.S. government estimates of nuclear damage. It is true that these effects all vary with conditions such as weather, time of day, terrain, the way the weapons are detonated, and the amount of shelter for humans. But just because effects can vary does not mean we can ignore them. Yet the U.S. government has done just that by relying almost exclusively on the effects of blast, thereby seriously underestimating the total lethality of nuclear weapons. There are, for instance, conflagration models estimating that deaths caused by fires would be 1.5–4.1 times greater than the government calculates. Overall, in my opinion, the U.S. government underestimates nuclear damage by a factor of at least two, and in some instances by one of eight, depending on the particular circumstance.* This amount of uncertainty as to the effects of nuclear detonations, plus the enormity of even the smallest of them, make it virtually impossible to develop plans for employing them with any precision.

Common sense tells us that it would have been difficult to employ the 32,500 warheads we once had in our arsenal, 13,000 of them being intercontinental range and each roughly thirty times as powerful as the bomb used at Hiroshima. The entire Soviet bloc had less than 250 cities with populations greater than 100,000, which would have meant fifty-two warheads per city. Needless to say, multiple nuclear detonations on the 250 largest population centers would damage those societies beyond recognition, just as Carthage was obliterated in 146 B.C. by Scipio Africanus, a Roman who not only conquered Carthage's army and razed the city but also placed a curse on its fields and sowed them with salt. The release of 13,000 nuclear warheads would, in effect, also sow salt in our own fields and those of many other nations because of contaminating radioactive fallout. The overkill this number of warheads represented was evident quite early. President Eisenhower commented back in 1959, when we had many fewer weapons, that military leaders were "trying to get themselves into an incredible position of having enough to destroy every conceivable target all over the world, plus a three-fold reserve."[5]

Because this was so obvious without any elaborate studies or calculations, the United States and Soviet Union decided in the early 1960s to

---

*A more detailed explanation of this contention is in Appendix A.

TABLE 2.1   Comparative Effects of Nuclear and Conventional Weapons, Nuclear
Weapons Airburst over an Urban Area (range in miles)

	Conventional 500-lb. Bomb	.1 KT (artillery shell)	12.5 KT (Hiroshima)	250 KT (U.S. ICBM)	550 KT (Russian ICBM)
Blast[a]					
Knock down unreinforced brick buildings	0.02	0.43	1	2.7	3.5
Thermal[b]					
Ignite wooden buildings	None[c]	.24–.34	.8–1.2	4–5	6–7
Radioactivity[d]					
Lethal to 50 percent of people exposed	None	5–10	15–30	50–100	75–150

[a]Nuclear blast ranges are computed assuming that the weapon height of burst has been adjusted to give 5 psi overpressure over the largest possible area.

[b]The ranges quoted here are for ten and twenty calories per square centimeter on the ground. At these ranges, fires will be initiated by the light-flash from the nuclear fireball.

[c]The blast wave from a 500-pound bomb could cause fires by knocking over stoves or by causing electrical shorts or broken gas lines. However, unlike a nuclear explosion, the bomb does not create a light-flash intense enough to set fires directly.

[d]In order for there to be significant fallout from a nuclear detonation, the explosion must occur on the ground or near the surface. The blast effects in the first row assume heights of burst that would not, in most circumstances, result in substantial early fallout. Depending on wind conditions, the actual distances where fallout from near-surface bursts could pose a serious threat of injury or to life could be larger or smaller. The downwind distances cited here should only be used as a means of establishing a rough scale of distance for serious fallout.

commence negotiating arms control agreements. Those agreements have brought us to the current objective of each having 3,000–3,500 warheads mated to delivery vehicles by 2003. One way to think about what 3,000 nuclear warheads could do to our nation is to hypothesize an all-out Russian attack distributed evenly among the fifty states (a conceptual strategy for illustrative purposes only). That means sixty warheads per state. Even if the warheads were distributed randomly, the impact would be unimaginable in Rhode Island and still a catastrophe in Alaska. And if the warheads were deliberately aimed at the sixty largest cities in each state, our country certainly would be another Carthage. Similarly, Russia today has roughly 200 cities with populations over 100,000; 3,000 U.S. warheads, or 16 per city, would carry it far past survival.

This is a worst-case scenario because it deliberately targets the most valuable assets: people and their places of work or living. There is an argument that attacking cities would be immoral. There is a counterargument that deliberately threatening cities and people would not be immoral, because it would make it so abundantly clear how disastrous nuclear war would be that deterrence would be reinforced. The world of nations has, however, been moving for almost a century toward outlawing the more horrific forms of warfare such as poison gas, biological toxins, and the indiscriminate killing of civilians. Nuclear attacks on cities would unquestionably fall into the category of horrific; therefore, developing plans to attack them deliberately could be more than our consciences would allow.

One alternative the United States has adopted, supposedly on moral grounds, is to target only military or military-industrial facilities, not cities. Curiously, this happens to accord with a doctrine enunciated more than 150 years ago by famed military strategist Carl von Clausewitz: The main target for an army is usually the enemy's army; that is, defeating the enemy's military forces is normally the best route to victory.[6] The idea of threatening only military targets also fits neatly with the thinking of many civilians involved in developing nuclear strategy. Their quest has been to find if there are ways to make using nuclear weapons acceptable. Any that destroyed too much would not be acceptable. For instance, President Eisenhower was so shocked because it was estimated that 285 million Russians and Chinese would die if our entire nuclear force was launched at them.[7] So to avoid such concerns with morality, civilians readily agreed to targeting largely military installations or military-related industries. Much of the early developmental work on such targeting strategies was done by a civilian group at RAND. Civilians like these play a much larger role in nuclear strategy than in conventional strategy because they need not defer to the experience and judgment of military officers. A former RAND analyst once stated it succinctly: "General, I have fought just as many nuclear wars as you have."[8]

But there is a problem with the military-target strategy: It demands many more weapons to pose a sufficient threat to deter. Essentially, it is the difference between aiming many weapons at military targets of modest value or a few weapons at civilian targets (i.e., cities) of great value. Besides, there are large numbers of military targets in countries like Russia and China, and being ready to destroy only a modest percentage of them would not necessarily intimidate sufficiently to deter. The most fundamental problem, however, is that many nuclear weapons aimed at military targets will inevitably damage cities and their residents.

There is a middle ground between the hypocrisy of pretending to target only military targets and the perceived immorality of targeting cities. Useful work on this was done at MIT in 1987 by a group under Dr. Kosta Tsipis, who employed a computer model of the U.S. economy to evaluate the effects of various sizes and kinds of nuclear attacks on the United States.* This group introduced hypothetical disruptions in economic activity as a result of attacks from nuclear weapons. The model was dynamic and reflected the secondary effects of the loss of the various activities destroyed. The study found that the United States is particularly vulnerable to attacks on the sources of and the distribution network for liquid fuel: refineries, oil fields, control centers for pipelines for gas and oil, and harbors. Some of these targets, like harbors, are clearly within cities; some, like refineries, oil fields, and key points in the pipeline systems, can be far away from population centers.

The simulation showed that as a result of 239 nuclear detonations aimed at the liquid fuel system, gross national product (GNP) returned to only 40 percent of the pre-attack level after six years; 60 percent of the population had died within two years. Both projections were largely the result of a breakdown of the nation's transportation network because of shortages of gasoline, diesel oil, and aviation fuel. Food supplies did not get through and people starved; components manufactured in one city for factories in other cities did not reach them; imported raw materials were prevented from reaching their destinations, which in turn slowed deliveries of other products; and so on down the chain. It is particularly noteworthy that the MIT study made numerous optimistic assumptions, for example, that the national communications system would remain sufficiently intact for the government to direct the recovery effort, and that national morale would hold up enough so that people would respond to directions.

The MIT approach meets the test of common sense. Just imagine the impacts if fuel was no longer readily available in U.S. cities. With electricity

---

*An excerpt from this study describing the methodology and results is included in Appendix B.

limited, workplace productivity would drop; with reduced availability of water, medical services, and sewage treatment, health would be endangered; and with limits on gasoline, public and private transportation would have to be curtailed with effects ranging from reduced supplies for factories to workers not being able to commute to garbage not being collected.*

The U.S. government's role in the MIT study is very telling. The dynamic model was developed by a private company on contract to the Federal Emergency Management Agency (FEMA), the organization responsible for civil recovery from nuclear attacks. As it became clear that the results from employing this model would undercut statements like that of Secretary of Defense Weinberger—that we could win a nuclear war— FEMA withdrew its support. The MIT group took over the model from the contractor and worked on it. When that group released its conclusions about the hypothetical attack of 239 weapons, FEMA repudiated it with a bland statement that the computer model was too sensitive to some economic variables, such as interest rates.[9]

The lesson from the MIT study is that the lasting impact of multiple nuclear detonations, upon an economy and a society, would be far greater than the sum of individual blasts. The ability of any urban area to recover from a nuclear attack would depend on outside assistance, as at Hiroshima and Nagasaki. But those sources of assistance could be attacked and require assistance themselves, which would prolong the recovery. Estimating such secondary effects is very difficult, but they are real. The 239 detonations in the MIT study could so protract the time it would take to restore our economy, government structure, and social institutions that when the society revived it would not be recognizable. Many democratic and humanitarian values could be set aside while we struggled with primary needs. If the nation's transportation net was crippled, the national economy might divide into regional economies. Our tightly integrated industrial economy might give way to a more agrarian one. Given regional agrarian economies, new internal political alignments would likely develop. And with medical resources severely overstrained, human relations

---

*The MIT thesis also accords with emerging academic attention to the theory of chaos and complexity. In essence, this says that as one factor goes wrong in a complex chain of related events, it distorts other factors and the end result is greater chaos than would appear warranted by the originating event. The U.S. military is just beginning to apply chaos and complexity theory to targeting problems.

could become uncivil. For instance, one sizable nuclear detonation over a major city could create more burn casualties than the capacity of all specialized burn facilities in the entire country could handle.[10] The greater the number of deaths, both instant and lingering, the more likely the psychological trauma would lead to despair and loss of will to recover. The prolonged struggle for basic survival and recovery could eclipse any substantive U.S. role in world affairs.

Society would have passed what we might term its *point of non-recovery*. Determining what amount of damage would constitute the point of non-recovery for the United States is, of course, a subjective matter. The 239 detonations on liquid fuel supplies, as in the MIT study, would seem to be sufficient. We need to pursue and refine such studies and not reject them out of hand if we are to make sensible decisions on nuclear policy.

Russia is also vulnerable to being pushed past a point of non-recovery. Russia is larger in area than the United States and, therefore, more dependent on transportation links, but those links rely on coal more than on liquid fuel. Russia's industry is not as highly developed as that of the United States and is concentrated in fewer locations. Whether threatening its transportation and communications systems would be the best approach to deterring Russia could also only be determined by doing specific, dynamic computer simulations. Still, there is no reason to suggest that some threat of about 250 warheads on some vital, national system would not put Russia into the category of being beyond the point of non-recovery.

China must also have a point of non-recovery, but that is more difficult to estimate. With its immense population and largely agrarian economy, China is less vulnerable than Russia and the United States to starvation and industrial interruption from a breakdown in transportation. China does have more limited transportation, electric power, and communications systems. Breakdowns in them could foster the breakup of the country into regional groupings as central authority became weakened. Again, specific simulations would need to be run, but China's vulnerability appears to be more political than economic. One possible indicator of China's thinking in regard to national vulnerabilities is that China has thus far limited the size of its nuclear forces that can reach the United States to less than fifty warheads and to central Russia to less than a few hundred. This could be the result of deliberate decisions to allocate limited high-technology resources elsewhere, but there are indicators the Chinese are more interested in qualitative improvements to their nuclear arsenal than to quantitative increases—that is, they apparently believe irreparable damage can be done to countries like Russia and the United States with only modest nuclear forces. Short of thorough study, it is not unreasonable to believe that about 250 nuclear detonations would also place China beyond the point of non-recovery.

Smaller nations are vulnerable to far fewer nuclear detonations because of the limited number of transportation, communication, and industrial systems. Their societies and economies could be drastically disrupted with relatively few nuclear detonations on key industrial plants, natural resources, and government. Perhaps the most limiting factor would be a moral question: Would there be enough targets outside of cities, or would any attempt to push them beyond the point of non-recovery be tantamount to attacking the entire society, including its population?

An MIT-type strategy of threatening vital national systems would not solve the moral problems of nuclear deterrence but would be morally preferable to a strategy of deliberate attacks on cities. It would also move us away from our fixation with the Clausewitzian dictum that defeating an enemy's military forces is the key to winning wars. That rationale has inflated our requirements for nuclear forces beyond reason and has led us into planning to wage nuclear wars in the image of conventional ones. It has also forced us to assume that if we are targeting Russia's nuclear forces they must be targeting ours and, hence, we must take the risks of being on hair-trigger alert lest they catch us by surprise. There is no element in U.S. nuclear policy more corrosive to rational policymaking than our adherence to the dictum that the objective in nuclear war must be to destroy the opponent's nuclear forces.

In addition, embracing an MIT-type strategy would remind us there is no need to threaten any nation all the way to extinction in order to deter. Threatening to push a nation past its point of non-recovery through attacks on various vital systems, such as liquid fuel supplies, should be more than adequate to deter or to do whatever amount of damage we might conceivably want to do. We need to study just what it would take to do that to various potential opponents. Whether it is specifically 250 or 500 or even 1,000 detonations is not important today, because all of those limits are far below our current target in START II of 3,500 warheads, let alone the 10,000 we intend actually to retain.

Alas, any suggestion that the United States needs only a few hundred nuclear warheads typically meets with vehement opposition. A standard objection is that we need to be prepared for more than one nuclear war. One example of this would be if we and the Russians each exhausted all of a limited number of warheads in a war with each other and the Chinese then stepped in and attacked either or both of us with nuclear forces. This is a case of extrapolating a possibility of conventional warfare to nuclear warfare without considering the order of magnitude of difference in the amounts of destruction. In this hypothetical situation, the United States and Russia, having pushed one another past their points of non-recovery, would need decades to rebuild economies, societies, and military power before being able again to threaten China or anyone else. Why would China want to engage either with nuclear weapons? It would already have been vaulted toward being the preeminent world power. For the sake of damaging us even more seriously, China would be taking an enormous risk as we might have just one surviving submarine with its load of missiles. China would be deterred because the potential gains would not be worth the risks.

Another objection to keeping only a minimum inventory of warheads is that we may need reserves in case a group of warheads deteriorates in peacetime or fails to perform in war. This argument is applicable only when the strategy requires hitting precise numbers of targets. When the strategy is to push an opponent past a point of non-recovery, a few detonations more or less are not significant. If we truly believed our retaliatory forces had deteriorated (and they never have in a significant way during the past fifty years) we would shift our targeting toward higher-value targets to ensure being able to threaten non-recovery. At the same time, we should keep in mind that the point of non-recovery is not precise. It is not like military targeting, where the difference between destroying 100 percent of an opponent's ICBMs, for instance, and only 90 percent could be vital. The MIT study concluded there would be a loss of 60 percent of the population after two years, but it would hardly make much difference if it turned out to be only 50 percent.

But the most fundamental reason for opposing a minimum inventory is a deep-seated concern with falling behind the Russians in any category of nuclear capability. The most strident voices are those expressing fear that our retaliatory forces could be overwhelmed: What if we went to 250 warheads and the Russians abrogated START II and retained, say, 7,000? Any reasonable person would be concerned with a 25:1 ratio, even if our retaliatory force was totally safe from attack. A 25:1 adverse ratio, however, is a bogus case. After all these years of focusing on parity in our negotiations on arms control and in our decisions on force levels, it would be politically impossible, let alone just plain imprudent, for us to allow such a wide differential to develop. At any reasonable ratio we have no cause to worry that the Russians could locate and destroy all of our nuclear forces before enough of them could launch a sufficiently devastating retaliatory attack to carry Russia to its point of non-recovery. (Just why this is so is discussed in Chapter 7.)

Concern with being overwhelmed, then, is more a stalking horse for a deep-seated conviction that superiority in these weapons affords us prestige on the world stage and political leverage over the Russians. Many nuclear strategists point to the Berlin crises of 1958 and 1963 as evidence that our nuclear superiority forced Nikita Khrushchev to back down. Yet they slight the fact that in the 1961 Cuban missile crisis President John Kennedy made concessions to the Soviets in spite of knowing that he was playing from a vastly superior nuclear hand.

In understanding whether there was nuclear leverage in cases like these, we need to differentiate between nuclear superiority and nuclear danger.[11] If Khrushchev was influenced by the nuclear imbalance, it was not because he feared his country would come out second-best in a nuclear exchange: It was because he knew his country would be devastated in the absolute, regardless of the relative amount of damage to the United States. Similarly, if Kennedy was unwilling to press his nuclear superiority, it was because his focus was on the absolute damage the United States might receive, not the much greater damage we could certainly do to the Soviet Union. In short, both leaders were deterred by the absolute danger their countries faced. Perceptions of nuclear superiority or inferiority did not afford leverage in those political showdowns.

What is important is to recognize that there is a cap on the number of nuclear warheads we might ever need. If we accept that concept, startlingly new opportunities for controlling nuclear weapons open up.

3

POINTS OF SELF-DETERRENCE

IN EARLY 1979, MAJOR GENERAL JASPER A. WELCH of the U.S. Air Force came to the CIA to brief me and several agency experts on arms control. The subject was the basing plan for the proposed MX ICBM. Ostensibly, the issue was how to locate the MX to make it less vulnerable than the current missiles, which were housed in highly visible concrete silos throughout remote areas of the United States. The general described the "racetrack" plan that had been selected by the Department of Defense after exploring some twenty alternatives, which included carrying the missiles in aircraft, placing them on railroads, hiding them in tunnels, and anchoring them on the bottom of the sea. In this plan we would build forty-three fixed shelters around oval, concrete tracks, each about twenty miles long and ten miles wide. There would be 200 separate tracks, all located in the deserts of Nevada. The individual shelters would be hardened with enough concrete so that a 1-MT nuclear weapon could destroy only the shelter it targeted. In just one of the shelters on each track there would be a single MX mounted on a wheeled transport vehicle.

The concept was to move the missile from one shelter to another between the time we detected an incoming missile attack and its arrival. This was all to be done automatically, that is, there would be no humans on the transporter. At the flip of a switch in a control center the transporter and its missile, weighing in at some 500,000 pounds combined, would move out and dash around the track. A guidance system embedded in the track would lead it to any of the other forty-two shelters. I was dumbfounded by this far-fetched scheme.

I was reviewing it because the president wanted to know whether making the MX safe from surprise attack in this manner might also make it impossible for the Soviets to check on the total number of MXs we had. The Soviet Union would be entitled under SALT II, the strategic arms limitation treaty that was then under negotiation, to use photographic satellites to verify the number of U.S. ICBMs. How would they be able to determine the number of missiles that were hidden in each set of forty-three shelters? Somehow we had to make our MXs both invisible and visible. General Welch told us the plan was to install large doors on top of the shelters and open them periodically during times Soviet photographic satellites passed overhead. After studying this, the CIA experts concluded the Soviets did have the ability to peer into these openings and ascertain whether a missile was housed there or not.

I had to bite my tongue in concurring with that evaluation because it would help this wild scheme move forward, but I could not resist chiding the general just a bit. Early in the briefing he had noted that to placate opposition from environmentalists, the Air Force would open the tracks to public use. They would be ideal for drag racing, he said. I asked, "What if there were people out there drag racing when that half-million-pound vehicle with nobody on board is suddenly launched out onto the track?" Unperturbed, he responded that any humans on the track might well be run over. He contended that it wouldn't matter in any event, because we would only launch that vehicle if we were convinced a Soviet nuclear missile was headed to that very track. Anyone on it was going to die anyway. I was nonplused at this prepared, coldly calculated response and at a loss as to what to say.

THERE IS A COMPULSION TO USE nuclear weapons, but because of their very power there is also a constraint. How could we ever have been serious about a scheme like the MX racetrack? It was certainly not because it would have improved the survivability of our ICBM force, as advertised. Yet when the Reagan administration took over the MX program two years later, the racetrack plan was replaced by one even more absurd. In "Dense Pack," 100 MX missiles would be clustered tightly together. An attack on any one would throw up so much debris as to destroy the follow-on attacking missiles aimed at the other ninety-nine. Presumably those ninety-nine would survive long enough to be launched after the debris had settled. This approach to being safe by inviting attack garnered the title "Dunce Pack." Congress laughed it out of being. Incredibly, we ended up placing MXs in existing silos, where they remain every bit as vulnerable as those they replaced.

This obsession with the MX, then, was not a quest for lesser vulnerability but one for a more powerful ICBM. That in itself conveyed the impression we wanted to enhance our capability for waging nuclear war because back then ICBMs were the best war-fighting nuclear weapons. They were unmatched in terms of carrying capacity, accuracy, and responsiveness to an order to shoot.* Our ICBM force, though, was inferior to the Soviets' in total amount of destructive potential. Despite the fact that nuclear missiles do not engage enemy nuclear missiles as, for instance, tanks fight enemy tanks, that discrepancy galled our nuclear strategists. Having the best war-fighting capability is seen as important because of the dictum of Clausewitz that "war is not a mere act of policy, but a true political instrument, a continuation of political activity by other means."[1]

If war is to be employed to further policy, political leaders must feel confident they will win. Historically, they have asked whether their military was capable of doing more damage to the opponent than the opponent to them, with particular emphasis on doing more harm to enemy military forces. When analyzing inside the nuclear sphere, however, political leaders ask a different question, as Khrushchev and Kennedy did during the Berlin and Cuban crises: whether the damage their country would receive in retaliation could possibly be acceptable. Pushing an opponent past its point of non-recovery two or three times would be without satisfaction if you are pushed there even once as a result. It is only common sense, then, that at some point prospective damage to oneself will inhibit the will to initiate the use of nuclear weapons. That point is identified as the *point of self-deterrence.*

The *point of non-recovery* defines the maximum number of nuclear weapons that a nation could usefully employ against another nation without going to excess. The *point of self-deterrence* defines the level of nuclear damage in retaliation that would deter a nation from initiating nuclear war.

---

*Technological developments have since made the sea-launched ballistic missile comparable in these categories of performance.

Points of self-deterrence will vary with a country's international position, objectives, culture, and form of government. During the Cold War we implicitly accepted the idea that it might be necessary to absorb considerable nuclear damage to the United States as a result of employing nuclear weapons in defense of European allies. As risky as this was, we believed this bluff was the most rational option we had. In the post–Cold War world, in contrast, our point of self-deterrence is as low as one nuclear detonation on our soil or against U.S. military forces overseas. There is no foreign policy objective today that is so threatened that we would employ nuclear weapons and accept the risk of receiving just one nuclear detonation in retaliation. We have only to look at the situations where the United States has made substantial military commitments since World War II:

- Western Europe: There is no longer a conventional military threat to our West European allies that they and we could not handle together.
- The Korean Peninsula: North Korea, with only one-eighth of the GDP of South Korea and one-half its population, although still a dangerous opponent, could not hope to win in any sustained combat.
- Vietnam: This country has long been off our list of vital concerns.
- The Mideast: The lesson of the Gulf War in 1991 is that we can protect our access to oil in the Mideast without deploying anything like the number of conventional military forces we sent there in 1990–1991.

Our initiating the use of nuclear weapons today in these or less vital situations would be highly questionable even if our actual point of self-deterrence was greater than one detonation. This is not to suggest that the United States will be paralyzed if it must confront a nuclear-armed adversary. We dealt with cautious firmness with the Soviet Union during the crises over Berlin and Cuba. Still, for nonnuclear powers who feel threatened by the United States today there is a premium on obtaining merely one or two nuclear weapons and the means to deliver them. We would, indeed, pause before intervening militarily against such a country. This is a fact of life that cannot be exorcised by not acknowledging it; it is already quite apparent to Third World nations. Note the statement, attributed to an Indian general following the Gulf War in 1991, that anyone planning to fight the United States had better possess a nuclear weapon.

There is, however, a more subtle point here: Our use of a nuclear weapon in confronting a nuclear power would almost certainly incite a nuclear response, whereas employing a conventional weapon might not. Of course, if we were able to destroy 100 percent of the adversary's nuclear weapons in one swift attack, it would be a different matter. Counting on that, however, would be very risky. No offensive weapons system can ever be so unfailingly reliable and accurate that we could be confident of destroying arsenals of hundreds or thousands of warheads—or even of locating all of a smaller arsenal, as when we failed to locate SCUD missiles and various nuclear, chemical, and biological facilities in Iraq during the Gulf War. In confronting a nuclear-armed adversary, then, a U.S. president would face three choices: employing nonmilitary means and gambling on being able to resolve the problem satisfactorily; intervening with conventional military force and gambling that this would not push the adversary into a nuclear response; and intervening with nuclear weapons and gambling on being able to totally blunt any nuclear retaliation. Not only is the nuclear alternative the most risky, it would carry far-reaching implications, such as breaking the fifty-year history of nonuse of nuclear weapons; I believe it would always come in a poor third.

Even without a threat of immediate nuclear retaliation, we would be inhibited from initiating the use of nuclear weapons. It is tempting to think we could safely initiate such use against a nonnuclear opponent. Clearly, there could not be immediate nuclear retaliation. Such an opponent might be cowed into conceding and then getting on with life. The kinds of opponents we would consider as worthy of an attack with nuclear weapons, however, are likely to be fanatics. Such an aggrieved nonnuclear victim might work doggedly to obtain a nuclear capability with which to exact revenge. Alternatively, resorting to terrorism, perhaps with chemical or biological agents, could be a more immediate alternative. Even if we avoided such consequences, we would have to answer to the international community for breaking the taboo on nuclear weapons; spreading radioactive contamination, real or imagined, perhaps beyond the country attacked; causing civilian casualties in that country; and applying overwhelming and disproportionate force. In weighing whether to accept these various risks, we would have to ask, "For what purpose?"

One commonly imputed purpose for our initiating the use of nuclear weapons is to deal with tyrants. Many believe we need the threat of maximum force to deter them. Nuclear weapons could, for instance, threaten them personally, even in deep, hardened bunkers, or one of their particularly important military units, like Saddam Hussein's Republican Guard, or their underground facilities for manufacturing weapons of mass destruction. Threatening might have its value but would be risky because it is doubtful we would ever follow through and use nuclear weapons for such purposes. In part we would be inhibited due to moral considerations. Detonating a sizable groundburst weapon on the middle of a major city such as Baghdad, literally to uproot a dictator like Saddam Hussein, could seem a disproportionate action to anything but the most egregious provocation. In part, we would be deterred by the unfathomable responsibility for opening a new nuclear Pandora's Box.

A frequently discussed reason for threatening the use of nuclear weapons against tyrants is to deter attacks with chemical or biological weapons. Supposedly, a veiled threat of nuclear retaliation by Secretary of State James Baker deterred Saddam Hussein from employing his chemical weapons during the Gulf War. There is a question as to whether Baker intended such a threat, and we will never know for sure what actually inhibited Saddam Hussein. The issue, though, is whether we would want to threaten nuclear retaliation to deter chemical and biological attacks in the future. A key reason not to is that it would encourage nuclear proliferation by demonstrating a utility for these weapons. If we need them for this purpose, how could we tell would-be proliferators like North Korea, Iraq, and Iran that they would not find them useful? Beyond that, we should not overlook the formidable threat our conventional military capabilities present. Countries that could be tempted into using chemical or biological weapons are likely to be vulnerable to sustained conventional attack. Finally, although it may seem cynical, we can likely have the benefits of threatening a nuclear response to chemical and biological attacks without actually doing so. Any tyrant considering the use of these weapons would know that no matter what we had said, our nuclear weapons could be brought into play with devastating impact. And the tyrant would have to worry that the American public might just demand such a response.

Another superficially appealing use for nuclear weapons against nonnuclear powers is to extricate ourselves from some difficult tactical situation in conventional war. Nuclear weapons are not very useful tactical instruments, however, when you consider their ancillary effects. They may irradiate territory into which your forces want to move; send radioactive fallout back onto your own forces or cities; and disrupt your own, as well as the enemy's, electronic environment. And even in their smaller forms they can easily be overkill, as tactical weapons come in fifteen sizes and all are large (as noted earlier, the smallest we had, a nuclear artillery shell, was the equivalent force of five B-2 bombers fully loaded with conventional bombs). General Colin Powell deprecated tactical nuclear weapons in his memoirs when discussing a plan he directed be prepared for employing them against the Iraqi army during the Gulf War: "The results unnerved me. To do serious damage to just one armored division dispersed in the desert would require a considerable number of small tactical nuclear weapons. I showed this analysis to [Secretary of Defense Dick] Cheney and then had it destroyed. If I had any doubts before about the practicality of nukes [nuclear weapons] on the field of battle, this report clinched them."[2]

General Powell also supported President George Bush's removal of almost all of our tactical weapons from deployed positions. In my experience, this aversion to tactical nuclear weapons is shared by most senior military officers, increasingly so since the mid-1980s. Still, specific arguments for using tactical nuclear weapons crop up regularly:

- One purpose would be to defend Saudi oil fields if, for instance, the Iraqis invaded Kuwait again and then thrust south. That would require Iraq to move sizable armored forces more than 200 miles across a desert using only a single highway. Well-trained and -maintained armored forces could do that, but it would be a logistical challenge that is almost certainly beyond Iraq's capabilities. Even if Iraq could pull it off, modest air or cruise missile attacks could disrupt movement across such open territory. Moreover, the Saudis and Kuwaitis would certainly prefer for us to use conventional munitions rather than nuclear weapons on advancing Iraqi forces inside their countries.
- Another scenario would arise in the U.S. response to a North Korean invasion of South Korea. North Korea has lost its allies and its access to their military technology; it is in desperate straits

economically; and its military forces, although large, simply cannot be well trained or supported. There is evidence, for instance, that pilots get fewer training hours in the air in one year than ours do in one month. Senior U.S. military officers do not question that we and the South Koreans could defeat such an invasion. The issue is whether we could prevent serious destruction to Seoul, which is within artillery range of the North Korean end of the demilitarized zone separating the two countries. There is no question that our nuclear artillery could be useful in silencing that artillery. Would the risk of unleashing weapons of a minimum equivalent of 220,000 pounds of TNT, which would generate radioactive contamination, in such a confined area be worth it? Or should we rely on massive conventional bombardment with aircraft and artillery, even though it might take longer and increase the risk to Seoul? The fact that we have withdrawn all nuclear weapons from South Korea, although they could be returned quickly, indicates that we do not see this as a vital use for these weapons.

- Still another possibility would be to conduct preemptive nuclear attacks to prevent the further proliferation of chemical, biological, and nuclear weapons. A problem here is whether our own public, let alone the world community, could be persuaded this was justified. Could we present conclusive intelligence that what was going on, indeed, was the manufacture of weapons of mass destruction? And even if we could, would there be enough to be gained to warrant unleashing the nuclear genie?

- Another possibility is a Russian invasion of its neighbors, such as Poland or Ukraine; or a Chinese invasion of its neighbors, such as Korea, Taiwan, or Japan. In any of these circumstances, the overriding consideration would be whether we would risk general nuclear war and the survival of our own society on behalf of those countries. If so, where would we stop short of becoming the world's nuclear policeman?

Another factor to consider is that we possess the most powerful conventional military forces in the world—an advantage that will likely continue for the foreseeable future. No other conventional military force comes close to ours in sophistication, both in equipment and in battle-field techniques. Moreover, no other force is as well trained to fight and logistically prepared to do so. If there are military challenges we cannot meet with U.S. conventional forces, they are at the low end of the spectrum, like jungle warfare or terrorism. Nuclear weapons would hardly be applicable. It is possible to conjure up hypothetical situations where the use of nuclear weapons could seem to be important. There should, however, for the foreseeable future be little reason to let ourselves get into them. It would be very difficult to explain to our own public, let alone the world, that we could not find some nonnuclear alternative. We would have to face the accusation that we had been seduced into leaning on our nuclear strength as a less expensive alternative, as with NATO in 1952.

The way in which we have downgraded tactical nuclear weapons in recent years is convincing evidence of our willingness to rely on conventional weapons. If we were ever to initiate the use of nuclear weapons, the odds are high that it would be with these smaller, tactical ones. Yet in 1991 we unilaterally withdrew all but a few hundred of them from bases in Europe and from all naval ships. Beyond that, we are voluntarily dismantling many tactical warheads, even before strategic ones.

Any nuclear power must consider the point at which it is self-deterred. It is often suggested that a "mad Russian" might be willing to accept more damage in retaliation than we would consider reasonable, and that is evidenced by Russia's historical perseverance in responding to invasions. Persevering, though, is different from taking a positive decision to accept the risks of heavy losses as a result of initiating nuclear war. And with the Soviet Union having collapsed in good measure because of economic insufficiency, Russians know they need to build economic strength rather than subject themselves to the possibility of nuclear destruction. To estimate the points of self-deterrence as one detonation for the United States and hundreds or even thousands for Russia is illogical. Since the end of the Cold War, the evidence is strong that Soviet leaders were quite realistic in understanding the unacceptability of nuclear damage. For instance, during a conversation I had with the Soviet Union's Marshal Sergei Akhromeyev in 1990, he made it clear he was under no illusions as to the utility of these weapons.

It is difficult to estimate China's point of self-deterrence, just as with its point of non-recovery. We simply know less of its leaders' views on nuclear matters, because we have not had the kinds of discussions with them we have with the Russians. Chinese industry is more concentrated than Russian or American industry, and nuclear destruction could seriously retard China's economic growth. However, it is possible China may well be less sensitive to nuclear damage because of its large population. We should make allowance for a somewhat higher point of self-deterrence, but hundreds or thousands seems unrealistic.

As for smaller nations that may become nuclear powers, points of self-deterrence will be very low since only a small number of nuclear detonations would push them past their points of non-recovery. The issue is whether any leader would be so fanatic as to accept considerable nuclear destruction in order to achieve some objective. Even fanatic leaders, if rational, must make a calculation of net benefits. If they anticipate a response that would push their country past its point of non-recovery, it is difficult to believe they would decide to use nuclear weapons. If leaders are irrational, there is no way to deter them from irrational acts, other than hoping that within their regime there will be others who will effect restraint. However, different values, rather than irrationality, may lead some leaders to stress some values, often religious or political, more than others. This, or a miscalculation, could lead to the use of nuclear weapons. It would likely be because a strong psychic benefit, such as an Arab state seeking to destroy Israel, overrode a rational estimate of the probability and extent of the likely retaliation. Thus, whereas the point of self-deterrence is logically low for such states, in some cases it may not be so in practice because the risks are not sufficiently clear.

There are also self-deterring forces working on terrorists. One is that the odiousness of a nuclear detonation could boomerang and lose them support were they identified with it. Also, an actual nuclear detonation would likely be overkill for most of their purposes. Still, because threatening a nuclear explosion in a major city has to be the ultimate in extortion, we cannot count on self-deterrence here.

The concept of a point of self-deterrence tells us, then, that in varying degrees nuclear weapons are self-regulating.

4

CONTROLLED RESPONSE

In JANUARY 1977, I WAS INVITED TO A MEETING of the Conference Board, a group of business leaders that gathers periodically to discuss issues of business. I was impressed with how knowledgeable and interested they also were on issues of national security. Obviously, they had brought in a military officer like myself because of that interest.

Surprisingly, I found considerable concern on their part as to the balance of U.S.-Soviet nuclear forces. They asked whether we were as far behind the Soviets as many feared. Did we need a larger ICBM to match the ones the Soviets had? Did not those large Soviet missiles make us vulnerable to a surprise attack? And did the Soviets' extensive program of civil defense shelters make them less vulnerable to our retaliation if they should attack us first?

It particularly intrigued me that business leaders would be so informed on a subject as out of the ordinary as civil defense. I had always been skeptical of civil defense programs. We had all seen that President Kennedy's effort to induce us to build home shelters and to vitalize a broad program of preparations for nuclear attack had failed. I had seen very little secret data on the Soviets' program but was skeptical.

Within two months of this meeting, I unexpectedly became Director of Central Intelligence. One of my early objectives was to make the CIA more open to the American public. The agency had just been through a series of investigations—with resulting widespread criticism. CIA needed to show Americans more of what it was doing on their behalf, within the limits of secrecy, of course. My plan was to produce more unclassified analyses on topics of interest to the public. Searching for a suitable topic for the trial run of this new policy, I recalled the Conference Board meeting and decided the issue would be Soviet civil defense.

It took time to persuade the professionals in CIA that it was a reasonable idea and worth their time. The result, however, was revealing: Only 10–20 percent of the urban population of the Soviet Union could be sheltered; primary reliance was on the evacuation of cities.[1] This was almost a charade. If the United States was to strike first, there would be no time for evacuation. If the Soviets were to strike first, they could not risk moving streams of people out of their major cities and thereby tip their hand. Moreover, in winter it would be unfeasible in places like Moscow. Protecting 20 percent in shelters might be nice for the leadership, but what kind of a country would they have left to lead? But even if no Soviets were killed, where would the people go and what would they do when they returned from evacuation or came out of their shelters into devastated cities? There would be nothing much left.

The evidence was there, however, that the Soviets were spending money and building shelters. On the one hand, it was futile and wasteful. On the other, it was a government doing what it could in case deterrence failed.

We should not assume we can deter indefinitely all use of nuclear weapons or contaminating devices. We need to think through what our response would be to varying types of nuclear attacks, starting with the worst (although least likely): a major attack that pushed the United States past non-recovery. Only Russia is currently capable of inflicting such damage, but we would have only one option in responding: Having little left to lose and not wanting the nuclear aggression to pay off, we would have to attempt to push Russia past its point of non-recovery. That means we must study what that would require, that is, what Russia's point of non-recovery is. Neither side, of course, would win. Hence, it is difficult to imagine what would lead the Russians to pursue such self-defeating aggression.

Some experts have argued that we would be deterred from launching any counterattack because doing so would invite even more destruction on the United States, that is, we would be pushed well beyond non-recovery, just as the Romans sowed salt in the fields of Carthage. This argument typifies one of the problems we have had with constructing nuclear strategy. It assumes we would be capable of a carefully calculated response amid an unimaginable calamity to our society. This would not be like losing a battle and regrouping to fight on; it would be losing a society and almost certainly tens of millions of people within a very short time. Who could possibly predict how we would react? We cannot even forecast who would survive to make decisions for the nation—or whether those in authority could even control our surviving nuclear forces enough to strike back. In short, we have developed nuclear strategies as though we were playing chess, without considering both the emotional and practical stresses induced by widespread nuclear destruction. What our next move would be after being pushed past our point of non-recovery is simply unpredictable.

Ironically, other nuclear strategists have argued that in the event of a major nuclear attack we must be prepared not only to push Russia past non-recovery but to attack every remaining Russian nuclear weapon so as to minimize further damage to ourselves. This assumes the Russians, having started a nuclear war, would allow their retaliatory forces to remain vulnerable. But chances are that they would either have confidence we could not locate them or would place them on alert in order to launch them upon detecting an incoming attack. Of course, we might catch some Russian weapons on their bases despite these precautions, but the likelihood of our being able to find and destroy many of Russia's nuclear forces is very small. Thus, this argument reveals yet another flaw in our strategic decision process: preparing for any possible contingency, no matter how slight the probability it will actually come to pass.

We need to think also about responding to lesser nuclear aggressions, from a single warhead to a relatively "modest" number. Currently, only Russia and China (excluding Britain and France) can deliver such blows, but eventually others will have this capability. Moreover, there is the possibility of limited nuclear attacks on other countries, including an attack on U.S. forces overseas, which could be delivered or caused by any existing or new nuclear power. There are a number of scenarios for such limited attacks.

Pure accident could be one cause. As noted earlier, we have had eleven accidents in which nuclear weapons were lost from U.S. aircraft and a number involving submarines loaded with nuclear weapons. The safety features that we built into the weapons prevented any detonations. We understand that the Soviets and now Russians have similar safety arrangements. Today, however, the startling deterioration of Russia's military plant, including nuclear-powered submarines rusting at their piers, forces us to wonder how well these precautions are being maintained. And the ongoing demoralization of Russia's military personnel has created the risk for mistake during training exercises that could result in the unintended launching of nuclear weapons. As far as the other existing nuclear powers, we know rather little of their accident records. Clearly, their military establishments can have accidents, just as we.

A second cause of limited attack could be from miscalculation. The United States has gone to nuclear alert more than 1,500 times without cause.[2] The chances of such incidents resulting in the unintended launching of a nuclear weapon have been low. In good part because we have always been skeptical of the evidence of an impending attack and in part because we understood the Soviets and Russians knew that neither of us could win by initiating nuclear war. But those calming ingredients might not exist between other national rivals, especially if there was proliferation of nuclear weapons or if, for instance, Pakistan and India went on nuclear alert against one another and began assembling nuclear weapons.

A third cause could be the unauthorized use of nuclear weapons. The United States has taken extensive precautions to prevent this. In some of our weapons systems, two keys must be turned nearly simultaneously to launch a nuclear weapon, and wherever feasible the keys are physically separated so that one person could not turn both. In others there is an electronic locking system whereby a coded message must be received and inserted into the locking device to unlock it.

However, some weapons have neither of these controls. For instance, in 1968, when I was in command of *USS Horne* (a guided-missile cruiser with nuclear warheads onboard), there was a requirement that two people—myself and the executive officer—certify to the officer with custody of the nuclear warheads that a message authorizing their release had been received and authenticated. That arrangement left room for a forceful and persuasive commanding officer to pressure subordinates into circumventing the rules. The strategic warheads in SSBNs have not had electronic locks either, although they are scheduled to be equipped with them by late 1997. Still, it is difficult not to believe that these various controls could not, with some ingenuity, be bypassed.

Our real protection is confidence in our personnel, that is, the low probability that enough people would deliberately try to circumvent the rules
to make it possible to do so. That might not hold up, however, if there was
consensus among personnel that communications with superior authorities had broken down and that releasing nuclear weapons quickly was vital
to the survival of the United States. Russia has had similar, perhaps even
more secure, systems of control over the release of nuclear weapons. But
again, we must question whether these will be enough if Russia's military
and political vicissitudes continue. British and French control systems appear to approximate ours. We know rather little about China's control system and less about those of Israel, Pakistan, and India because these three
nations, which do not acknowledge having nuclear weapons or the potential for assembling them, do not discuss such matters.

What is most worrying, however, is whether rogue states that acquire
these weapons would establish good controls. On the one hand, dictators
are wont to retain a firm hand over their military. On the other hand,
there are greater risks of fanatics in the military establishments of rogue
states. One specter is that of a group of fanatic Arab officers feeling justified in launching a weapon at Israel; another is fanatics from any nation
with deep, historical rivalries wanting to take advantage of a newfound
nuclear edge.

And finally there is the chance for deliberate use. In my opinion, it is in-
conceivable that the United States, Britain, or France would initiate nuclear war. Historically, Russia and China have not been inclined to do so,
either. We cannot rule this out, however, in light of the uncertainties as to
the types of leadership and political structures these two countries will
develop in the future. The threshold nuclear powers could be tempted to
employ nuclear weapons in self-defense against a conventional assault
that threatened their survival, although Pakistan and India would have to
consider that their opponents, India and China, respectively, are more
heavily armed nuclear powers.

In sum, with the existing nuclear powers there will always be the risk of
the use of nuclear weapons, but short of major changes in the world's political climate this is a low probability. But what of new nuclear powers? A
principal concern is that one of the rogue states might obtain a nuclear
capability before its rival and attack while it had that advantage. We also
must be concerned that fanatics could attack anyone, including larger nu-

clear powers. Some leader with a nuclear weapon might find a psychic satisfaction in damaging Israel, or Russia, or China, or the Great Satan of the
United States that would offset any retaliation by the victim. Fanatics
might also miscalculate the resolve of the nation being attacked and expect to avoid any retaliation, or they might believe they could disguise
their attack and escape undetected. In sum, we would consider a fanatic's
attack on a major nuclear power as irrational, but it certainly cannot be
ruled out. Terrorists are another matter, since they have no territory to
speak of that is vulnerable to counterattack. Fortunately, as far as we
know, terrorists have not demonstrated serious interest in obtaining nuclear devices. Still, the planting and detonating of crude nuclear devices
by terrorists cannot be ruled out.

The normal maxims of warfare are not applicable in the context of limited nuclear attacks. In thinking through how to respond, we face the
dilemma of needing to use military force while suppressing the normal military instinct to use it as forcefully as capabilities permit. In military jargon
the objective is to establish a "favorable exchange ratio," that is, if your opponent does one unit of damage to you, you must do two or three to him.
Theoretically, that should wear down your opponent's will to continue. A
favorable exchange ratio does not guarantee victory, but military leaders
will almost always seek one. For instance, when the 1994 Nuclear Posture
Review called for our retaining 10,000 nuclear warheads rather than 3,500,
it was presumably to let us fight it out with the Russians. We would certainly
feel compelled to do something if attacked, but almost anything we could
do would bring unacceptable damage on us in retaliation.

One precaution would be to ensure that we do not panic when facing
nuclear detonations. Over the past fifty years we have come too close to
mistakes and accidents as a result of being on hair-trigger alert. Thus, it is
essential that we have nuclear retaliatory forces that are so secure that we
need not fear their destruction before we can use them. There are two approaches to invulnerability: numbers and stealth. In the 1940s and 1950s,
we turned to numbers of bombers. Since the early 1960s, we have relied
on numbers of ICBMs and bombers and on stealth in submarines. Today,
as both we and the Russians reduce numbers through mutual agreement,
we are implicitly rejecting security in numbers. The ICBM does not have
many other virtues. Even worse, it has the major disadvantage of making
it appear that we intend to take the offense. We deny that, but anyone sit-

ting in a vulnerable ICBM silo understands that firing first will very likely be necessary to achieving the mission. Another disadvantage is that the sense of vulnerability of ICBMs has prompted us to adopt the risky procedures of high alert, such as being ready to launch thousands of missiles with only a few minutes' warning. However, the ICBM is not nearly as vulnerable as our precautions suggest. The probability of Russia being able to coordinate a perfect, near-simultaneous attack on even a modest force of ICBMs is very low. Enough of them would surely survive, and so the Russians would be self-deterred. The ICBM, then, is a liability because of its image of vulnerability. That is what drives us to large numbers and risky readiness procedures that appear to favor taking the offense.

The second most vulnerable element of our nuclear forces is the bomber leg. Bombers, however, can be moved among bases and even launched as a precaution and then recalled, and so they are less of a liability than ICBMs. As a practical matter, our country is going to maintain a force of high-performance bombers for conventional missions. The marginal cost of retaining some of them in a dual nuclear role would be small.

The least vulnerable forces by far are the Navy's strategic ballistic missile submarines. Their disadvantages are that they are expensive and that they carry so many warheads in one platform (normally 192). We could ameliorate costs by shifting some of the burden of invulnerability to the Navy's force of attack submarines (SSNs). In a mix of SSBNs with sea-launched ballistic missiles and SSNs with sea-launched cruise missiles (SLCMs), the attack submarines would be virtually free of cost because the Navy expects to maintain forty to fifty SSNs for conventional warfare anyway. A few cruise missiles could be accommodated in some or all of them without serious penalty. These cruise missiles would also be a hedge against an effective antiballistic missile defense system because they are air-breathing rather than ballistic.

There are two solutions to having too many warheads in one platform: (1) decrease the number of warheads per submarine and increase the number of submarines at additional cost; or (2) spread sea-based retaliatory capability across both types of submarines. Having more platforms is also a hedge against a breakthrough in submarine detection techniques, although concern over this has been considerably overplayed. In the extreme, even if submerged submarines become fully visible they would still be better than fixed ICBMs, which are not only visible but do not move. Submarines are likely to become more visible, but a break-through to full visibility is unlikely. We and the Russians have dedicated immense efforts for more than fifty years to detecting submarines, and almost every gain has been offset by countermeasures. Moreover, detection of a single submarine is only the beginning. A nuclear aggressor would have to count on being able to knock out an entire force and before any of them could launch retaliatory attacks. Destroying such a force nearly simultaneously would be a formidable task. Thus, although we should not ignore the possibility of increased vulnerability of submarines, the precaution of backing them up with even more vulnerable ICBMs has never made sense.

Dispensing with ICBMs as numbers of weapons decrease overall is inevitable; even many within the Air Force would agree. Yet it will be difficult politically to tip the balance of strategic nuclear forces decidedly toward the Navy, that is, placing most of our strategic retaliatory forces in SSBNs and SSNs. Somehow we will have to break the enshrined concept of a TRIAD of strategic forces consisting of ICBMs, bombers, and SSBNs. More than one system is desirable, but there is no magic in possessing these three: The most desirable mix—bombers, SSBNs, and SSNs—is a TRIAD also. It would give us the best assurance we need of being able to retaliate against any nuclear aggression without panic.

The next question is how we should react if deterrence does fail. There are three options: (1) not respond; (2) respond at or above the level of destruction of the aggression; and (3) respond at a lower level:

- Not to respond would invite more nuclear aggression; for a very small or perhaps accidental attack, however, it could serve as a prudent brake on escalation.
- To respond by exchanging blows until one side capitulates would invite more nuclear destruction on the United States, regardless of whether we "won" by doing more damage to the opponent. The exception to this is the unlikely event that our retaliation completely disarmed the aggressor's remaining nuclear capability.
- To respond at a lower level, rather than escalate, might encourage the aggressor to call a halt to the use of nuclear weapons and attempt to resolve differences by other means before matters got out of hand. McGeorge Bundy, in a seminal book on nuclear

policy, favored what he termed the "less-than-equal reply." He pointed out that "there is a compelling difference between having a survivable capacity for destruction, and a decision to inflict that destruction after deterrence has failed."[3]

There are unconventional ways to respond to limited nuclear attacks with "less-than-equal" forcefulness:

- Attacks on a number of the aggressor's most valuable facilities, governmental or industrial, could be made with nuclear weapons delivery systems carrying dummies (e.g., lead weights instead of warheads). Dropping several of these into the Kremlin, for instance, would do limited damage but send an unmistakable signal as to what could come next. We would, of course, have to design and manufacture these special warheads and have them ready to mount.
- High-altitude nuclear bursts designed to produce EMP could be directed at urban-industrial areas. These could temporarily knock out industrial operations, with no other physical destruction and only limited deaths due to outages of electricity. These bursts could be sustained for periods of time to reinforce the message as to how vulnerable the aggressor's society is. The psychological impact alone could be considerable. Again, this is an option that would require advance design, production, and operational planning. For instance, in order to avoid unwanted electronic effects on our satellites in space, we would need to install special shielding on the upper hemisphere of the weapon and plan for a combination of weapon yield and altitude of burst that would minimize energy escaping into space.
- Precision attacks with conventional or nuclear weapons could be made on a sizable number of important industrial facilities, such as power plants and key points in communications and transportation systems. These would minimize deaths but indicate how fragile the industrial structure is.
- Any of these limited responses could be misinterpreted by the aggressor and trigger further attacks. To avoid this we would want to attempt to communicate to the aggressor that we were

launching a limited response and that it would be a good idea to ride it out and then negotiate.

These kinds of options for retaliating to a limited nuclear attack could be called a *doctrine of controlled response*. Just how "controlled" these responses became would be a function of the nature of the nuclear aggression and the psychology of the aggressor. For instance, in the case of a limited attack by Russia on the United States, we would select controlled options against the Russian homeland. If the attack were against U.S. forces overseas, we might use options against Russian military forces either at home or abroad. For limited nuclear attacks by smaller countries, either on the United States or U.S. forces overseas, controlled response options like EMP bursts could be particularly appropriate, for a single burst could easily blanket many countries. In the case of clandestine nuclear attacks on the United States by either an unidentified small nuclear power or terrorist groups, nonlethal or minimally lethal controlled responses on the primary suspects could be an alternative to doing nothing.

Perhaps the most cogent objection to the doctrine of controlled response is that simply discussing less than fully lethal responses to a nuclear attack weakens our deterrent threat. It is an axiom of conventional war that deterrence is a function of both military power and the will to apply that power. In other words, possessing the force alone will not deter your adversary if it believes you do not have the will to employ that force. However, this axiom is not applicable in the context of nuclear deterrence. Any nation considering aggression against the United States could not help but recognize that our overwhelming nuclear power could end their society. To gamble that we did not have the will to use it, no matter what the stated policy, would be an enormous risk. In short, deterrence is the product of two factors: the force available and the will to employ it. When the force is immense, the factor of will does have a significant impact on the product.

How likely is it that a controlled response would induce an opponent not only to cease nuclear aggression but to capitulate by making reparations and opening its nuclear establishment to international supervision? An aggressor, knowing that ultimately we have greater power, would either have been desperate or have made a tremendous miscalculation. It is possible, then, that a controlled response could provide a much-needed opportunity for the aggressor to reassess matters. Controlled response is not something a president could decide on easily, because there would be public pressure to punish any nuclear aggressor severely, and there is good reason to question whether a controlled response would accomplish all we want. Still, the alternatives are not attractive, and we need not rush into war-fighting if we have invulnerable retaliatory forces (e.g., SSBNs and SSNs). We could try controlled response without losing the option to respond more forcefully later on.

The three major concepts discussed thus far—*point of non-recovery, point of self-deterrence,* and *controlled response*—together offer a new theoretical foundation for our nuclear strategy. The old strategy, whatever its merits, led us to produce inordinate numbers of these weapons, a willingness to accept great risks in maintaining weapons in conditions of high alert, and war plans that reached such astronomical lengths that no individual could comprehend them. Not many of those who wrote those million pages of war plans believed they would work. Not many who organized the alert procedures believed such plans were wise. Not many who did the analyses that proved we needed 32,500 nuclear warheads believed in anything close to that number. And not many who estimated the extent of probable damage in our war plans believed the United States or Russia could survive the consequences of a nuclear exchange. Some played these games for the intellectual challenge; some played to enhance the parochial interests of a military service or an industry. The more serious and intelligent participated in making these plans because they believed the only way to deter nuclear war was to have the plans and the capabilities to carry them out.

With the end of the Cold War, our sizable edge in economic, political, and military power places us in a favorable position to question whether we need to go to such extremes in order to deter convincingly. During the Cold War, with a sense of imminent threat, it would have been difficult to change strategies that, although risky, were working. Today, we can afford to experiment with more consistent premises and then attempt to lead the other nuclear powers into adopting them. Russia's economic plight will make it difficult to resist our lead; witness that in 1991, when it became clear a choice needed to be made between guns and bread, the Russian military establishment, including some of its nuclear forces, began to crumble. The British and the French might resist changes in nuclear doctrine, but intensive consultations should bring them along. China's response would be difficult to predict, but it has never adopted some of our most pernicious theories, such as the importance of nuclear parity and the advantages of initiating nuclear war.

The time is ripe, then, to discard many of the past premises of our nuclear strategy. Doing so would open new possibilities for nuclear stability.

Part Three

The Solution

5

STRATEGIC ESCROW

In October 1990, I visited Moscow as a private citizen, a tourist. I did, however, request a meeting with Marshal Sergei Akhromeyev, former chief of the Soviet general staff and at the time a key adviser to President Mikhail Gorbachev. At 8:00 P.M. one evening a black limousine picked me up at my hotel and drove me through a towered gate into the courtyard of the Kremlin. I was escorted up a broad staircase and down a long, empty corridor with lots of doors but no decoration. The room I was ushered into was sparse as well, with only a modest bare table, a few chairs, and a map of the world on one wall.

In a few moments the marshal, a slim, balding man in uniform with a myriad of decorations, came in. His eyes were penetrating, but he exuded friendliness. It was to be just the two of us and an interpreter. As fellow military men, we quickly found grounds for discussion. He started by berating me for the threat our Navy's aircraft carriers posed to his country. I replied that those carriers were useful in many places, but we would never risk sending them close enough to the Soviet Union in wartime to be a serious threat.

I then took my turn to suggest that we both knew our countries had far too many nuclear weapons. Akhromeyev flashed an instant "Da," almost before the translator stopped. I next suggested he persuade President Gorbachev to dispose unilaterally of any 10,000 of their weapons to get the ball rolling. I added that President Bush would almost be forced to follow suit because the American public would want to afford neither the expense nor the risks of retaining more of these weapons than we needed.

Akhromeyev was cool to the idea and said the United States would have to go first. I pointed out that I was a lonely voice on this in the United States and was not in a position of authority. He was better placed to plant the seed. He dropped the issue and moved on.

About forty-five minutes later in our dialogue I came back to this idea. Akhromeyev was more contemplative and ended this second discussion by saying that maybe it was a good idea. Another forty-five minutes later, as the meeting was drawing to a close, he leaned over and asked, "Would you mind if I used your idea about 10,000 warheads with Gorbachev?" I parted feeling great warmth for the man and a ray of hope for the idea.

Ten months later Akhromeyev was dead. There had been an abortive coup attempt against Gorbachev. Whatever Akhromeyev's involvement, when it was all over he had taken his own life. If START II is implemented by 2003 as scheduled, each side will have reduced its strategic warheads by about 10,000. I will always wonder whether, in the absence of the political machinations going on within the Kremlin, Akhromeyev might have been able to lead both countries to those reductions perhaps five to ten years earlier.

IF PARITY WITH RUSSIA IS NOT ESSENTIAL, there are new opportunities for controlling nuclear weapons. We need not be limited by the painfully slow process of arms control agreements. We could take a leaf from one of the most successful efforts ever to limit nuclear arms. In September 1991 President Bush, using his authority as commander in chief, simply ordered almost all of our tactical nuclear weapons withdrawn from forward land bases and from all naval ships. Soviet President Mikhail Gorbachev responded with similar actions almost immediately.

A corresponding initiative with strategic nuclear weapons would be for us to remove perhaps 1,000 warheads from operational strategic launchers and place them in *strategic escrow*,[1] that is, in designated storage areas some distance from their launchers. We would invite the Russian Federation to place observers at each storage site. Their duties would be limited to counting the number of warheads going into storage, keeping track of whether any were moved, and conducting surprise inventories to ensure none had been clandestinely removed. They would also be allowed to check that other warheads had not been placed on the launch vehicles from which those in storage had been removed. These observers would have no authority to prevent our removing any or all warheads from any storage facility. They would, however, warn Moscow if we did.

The hope is that the Russians would follow our example, as before. If they did not, there would be no risk. We would still be at parity with the Russians in numbers of warheads, even if 1,000 of ours would have to be returned to and remounted on their launch vehicles before use. That is hardly a serious concern considering that even in 2003 with an inventory of 3,500 we will have so many more operational warheads than we could possibly employ usefully.

If the Russians did follow our lead, it would open the door for a rapid series of initiatives and reciprocations by both parties. There would be no need for protracted negotiations while quibbling over details. There would be no need for parliamentary approvals, though both presidents would need to build support in their legislatures. Both would want to point out that because the warheads would all be intact neither would have fewer than the other at any time. Moreover, there would be no violation of the U.S. Senate's reservation on START II that the president not let an imbalance develop that "could endanger our society."

At the same time, this would be a more meaningful step than the detargeting and de-alerting procedures we and the Russians have instituted in recent years, as reconstitution would take days or weeks, not minutes or hours. And the president would not have to obtain a two-thirds vote in the Senate, as with any treaty. There would be no need to hammer out detailed rules for verification for escrow, as all that would be required would be straightforward counting of numbers of warheads going in and out. Cheating by placing elaborately faked warheads in storage would theoretically be possible, but there are technical devices being developed that will counter such a ploy. In addition we need not be concerned that the Russians would gain significant intelligence about our weapons from looking at warhead casings.

If we made the second increment of warheads perhaps 2,000–3,000, this process could gain real momentum. From the early 1997 levels of about 8,000 operationally ready warheads, both we and the Russians could be down to a number like 1,000 well before START II's 3,500-warhead target for 2003, or even the much-discussed 2,000-warhead target, which could result from a START III at some date thereafter.

Once this process of strategic escrow through initiatives and reciprocation was well established, either side could move in a number of directions:

- Observers from the other side could be positioned at all storage
  sites for reserve warheads and arrangements made to store reserve
  warheads at some distance from the weapons systems to which
  they could be mated; for example, ICBM warheads could be
  moved to storage sites on a strategic bomber base rather than at
  an ICBM complex, thus meaning it would take some time to move
  and mate them to delivery vehicles.
- Observers could also be placed at storage sites for all tactical
  warheads on each side. With tactical weapons it would be
  important to locate the storage separately from the delivery
  systems (e.g., siting warheads for air-launched cruise missiles on a
  submarine base rather than on an airfield where the delivery
  aircraft are located). Most importantly, the United States would
  want to move its aircraft-launched tactical nuclear warheads in
  Europe back to the United States. There would be little at risk
  here, as both sides have shown their disdain for the utility of these
  weapons (the Bush-Gorbachev moves of withdrawing almost all
  of them from forward positions). This would have the added
  advantage of placing Russia's tactical nuclear weapons under
  better scrutiny. These weapons may be classified as "small," but
  rogue nations and terrorist groups would be delighted to buy or
  steal such "small" weapons.
- Components, such as guidance sets from the weapons or
  plutonium pits from the warheads, could be removed and placed
  at separate storage sites to further complicate and delay
  reassembly. This process could be reversed if one side did not
  follow.
- The casings of some warheads in storage could be deliberately
  damaged to the point that they could be remounted on delivery
  vehicles only with a complete reworking. Even this would not
  result in either side having fewer weapons than the other; they
  would simply be less accessible.
- Warheads could be dismantled. For the time being we should
  delay this, as it results in a residue of enriched uranium or

plutonium. Until there is greater assurance of firm control over all elements of Russia's nuclear programs, it will be preferable to store entire warheads rather than such fissionable materials, which are more readily pilfered. In addition, Russian fissionable material is under the control of a civilian agency, Minatom. However, the Russian military, which has better security than Minatom, controls warheads.

- Some international agency could be invited to install observers at all storage sites. This would give the rest of the world more confidence that the reductions called for in the NPT were actually taking place. There could be a suspicion of U.S.-Russian collusion to deceive the world. Besides, it will be important to prepare for the day when numbers get so low that the other nuclear powers must become involved. The International Atomic Energy Agency (IAEA) of the United Nations (UN) would be a logical candidate, but its skills are more in the control of fissile materials than warheads and components. Also, there is no way to exclude rogue states from providing the IAEA with inspectors in order to learn whatever they could about the U.S. and Russian nuclear programs. A new organization or new ground rules for the IAEA would need to be arranged.

When we and the Russians reach a level of about 1,000 warheads each, it will be time to pause in this escrow process. The accomplishment of getting there in just a few years would be of great significance, as the numbers of immediately usable nuclear weapons would have been dramatically reduced. This would ease one of our greatest concerns about proliferation: the uncertain and poorly supervised conditions in Russia's nuclear establishment. It would start both countries on the road to considerable cost savings. It would send a signal to American and Russian citizens and the rest of the world that we were serious about caging the nuclear genie. Still, this would only be "Phase 1," because even 1,000 warheads would leave both societies at risk. The informal arrangement of initiatives and reciprocation would no longer be an adequate basis for proceeding further. Although up to this point verifying what was placed in escrow would be adequate, the number of warheads remaining would now become important.

The next step, then, would be to negotiate a Phase 2 that would organize how to continue downward from 1,000 deployed, ready warheads to zero. Since the United States and Russia would, soon after reaching 1,000, approach the arsenal levels of France, Britain, and China, Phase 2 would have to be organized on a multinational basis. It would be desirable to bring in Israel, Pakistan, and India sooner rather than later. The fact that the United States and Russia had actually achieved levels of about 1,000 warheads would go far toward pressuring all six of the other nuclear or threshold nuclear countries to join the process. There is another inducement: Under a strategic escrow program none of them would have to give up their nuclear weapons, at least initially. French pride, for instance, would be assuaged because France would only have to place weapons in a less operational condition.

Arranging for the necessarily intrusive, multinational verification procedures would be one task of the Phase 2 negotiations. Before any nuclear power would place all of its warheads in escrow, it would insist on assurance that all other nuclear powers were doing so also. One beauty of escrow, however, is that the weapons are retrievable. Storage could be arranged so that even when the total number of warheads left in inventory was small, say, 200, it would take so much cheating to expose them all to a surprise attack that it would be readily detectable (e.g., with only 200 warheads in escrow, they could be stored so that it would take anywhere up to 200 attacking warheads to destroy them all; with only a few SSBNs kept at sea there would be no risk that all launch vehicles could be destroyed). Besides, if at any time a Russian preemptive attack appeared to be feasible, we would simply remount some warheads on SSBNs and keep them safely at sea until the situation was clarified.

Another task of Phase 2 would be to establish an ultimate, permanent level of warheads and launchers. To get below the points of non-recovery of the three principal nuclear powers, but still have enough to make preemption difficult, a target of about 200 of each would be logical. That would require detailed procedures for verified dismantling of all other warheads and launch vehicles. It would be a complex, difficult negotiation, but by conducting the Phase 2 negotiations concurrently with the execution of Phase 1 we could hope that when Phase 1 was complete the terms for Phase 2 would be ready.

The endpoint of a program of strategic escrow, then, would be:

- All nuclear warheads in the world in internationally supervised storage at some distance from their launchers.
- A limit of not more than 200 warheads and accompanying launchers for each nuclear power.
- Observers to provide warning of any effort to mate warheads to launch vehicles.

There are three principal impediments to getting a process of strategic escrow off the ground: whether the United States would be willing to start it; whether Russia would be willing to reciprocate; and whether there would be sufficient commitment on both sides to find the resources to carry it out.

Just a few years ago, our fixation with numerical parity and our ingrained distrust of Russia would have made the unilateral initiatives of a strategic escrow program politically unfeasible. One concern would have been the possibility of an overwhelming surprise attack should the Russians gain a numerical advantage. Phase 1, however, would not create any meaningful disparity in numbers, just temporary disparities in readiness. Beyond that, we should never forget that our ballistic-missile submarine force is a more than adequate secure deterrent to any such attack. The question is whether the U.S. president and congressional leaders will set aside political concerns enough to give the slow process of arms control a bold jump start. The key feature of a program of strategic escrow is that once started it would very likely gain momentum. As both sides placed warheads in storage, they would appreciate how excessive they had been by keeping tens of thousands. And if someone later suggested remounting warheads from storage, it would be difficult for them to explain why that should be done.

Some Russian leaders would likely be opposed to the limits related to strategic escrow because they see their nuclear capabilities as compensating for their decline of power. Financial realities may very well provide the impetus, however. The Russian military is already being forced to downsize because of a lack of resources. Bearing the cost of maintaining larger nuclear forces than the United States will appear less and less attractive, especially when nuclear forces cannot be used to solve problems like those in Chechnya. Pique and pride may still stir some voices to argue for a larger nuclear arsenal, but they will be out of tune. For instance, during the negotiations for START II, it was President Boris Yeltsin who pro-posed a level of only 2,000 warheads. And as my conversation with Mar-shal Akhromeyev evidenced, informed Russians understand that lower numbers are inevitable and desirable. Our strengths permit us to move voluntarily toward lower numbers; Russian weaknesses will force them to follow in time.

The most serious constraint would be a lack of storage space. The num-ber and location of available storage facilities for nuclear weapons in the United States are kept secret. It is difficult to believe, however, that in a system as large as ours has been, there would not be space immediately available for several thousand extra warheads to get Phase 1 started. We would then need only 3,000–5,000 additional storage spaces, and we are already dismantling warheads at a rate of about 1,500 per year, which in itself opens up storage. We can also shift storage around as suggested above by, for example, placing one kind of warhead in storage facilities for another so as to separate warheads from their launch vehicles. I doubt it would be necessary, but we might have to rehabilitate or expand old stor-age sites or even build new ones. The construction would be simple: con-crete bunkers suitably spaced, with some maintenance facilities in which to conduct checks on safety and operational readiness. There could, of course, be objections from citizen's groups, and requirements for environ-mental impact statements could impose delays.

Russia would have a larger problem. Under the Cooperative Threat Re-duction Program,* we are already financing the construction of storage facilities at Mayak, Russia, for fissile materials removed from Russian war-heads now being disassembled. Conditions in Russia are so chaotic that this and other parts of the same program have been beset with frustration

---

*The Cooperative Threat Reduction Program, or Nunn-Lugar Program, is a congressional initia-tive that began in November 1991. It grants the U.S. Department of Defense the authority to fund as-sistance to Russia, Belarus, Kazakhstan, and Ukraine to dismantle and destroy weapons of mass de-struction; to strengthen security for nuclear weapons and fissile materials; to prevent proliferation; and to help demilitarize the industrial and scientific infrastructure that has supported weapons of mass destruction in the newly independent states. The program makes available the U.S. assistance necessary to encourage the eligible states to undertake the dismantling of weapons of mass destruc-tion. One goal of the program was to assist Belarus, Kazakhstan, and Ukraine in becoming nonnu-clear states; that has been achieved. The other goal is to assist Russia in accelerating strategic arms re-ductions to START I and II levels.

and delay. For instance, despite our help, the Russians are still complaining about the costs of downsizing their nuclear arsenal. We would likely have to contribute funds to expand the Mayak facility or to construct adequate facilities for the storage of Russian warheads elsewhere. Whether Congress would fund this is an open question. With ingenuity, there are multinational opportunities to keep costs down:

- We could reduce the size of the storage requirement by removing and storing plutonium pits rather than complete warheads, for instance. That, however, would be less desirable than storing warheads, as it would be less of an impediment to rebuilding and less of a symbol of the downgrading of nuclear weapons.
- We could look for storage sites outside Russia where there would be fewer bureaucratic delays and where our Congress might be less reluctant to make an investment. In this event, we would have to store ours in the same general area as well. Norway and Sweden are two possibilities. They are close to Russia, have sizable, remote, lightly populated areas, and as they are strongly antinuclear they could be called upon to take on this temporary burden to reduce the threat of nuclear weapons. There are other possibilities: Greenland; a South Pacific atoll, such as Muroroa, where the French conducted nuclear tests; and aboard ships anchored in a remote area.

At the most, there would probably be something on the order of a few thousand warheads that could not be squeezed into existing facilities. It will be a problem, but not an insuperable one. There are no technical issues. It is only a matter of our political will to get it done.

6

NO FIRST-USE

In September 1975, I was appointed commander in chief of NATO's southern flank, based in Naples, Italy. The responsibilities of this command included the defense of Italy, Greece, and Turkey from invasion by land. Being a naval officer, I needed to learn a good deal about the tactics of ground warfare. One concern that intrigued me about land defenses was how we would stop an assault into northern Italy. An approach the Warsaw Pact could take would be to drive from Eastern Europe across Austria and south over Brenner Pass through the Alps. I assumed we had a good chance of disrupting such a large-scale movement in the mountains but wanted to know just how. I decided to start by talking with Colonel John B. Keeley of the U.S. Army, a good friend whom I knew to have an imaginative approach to such problems. Just before coming to the staff of the southern flank, John had commanded the 2nd brigade of the U.S. Army's 3rd Armored Division. This brigade was positioned astride Fulda Gap, the principal invasion route from Eastern Europe into West Germany. Although the terrain at the gap was different from that at Brenner Pass, I wanted to talk to John about defense of passes and gaps.

John described the tactics he and his superiors had envisioned for plugging the Fulda. He mentioned they included atomic demolition munitions (ADMs) to blow up a hillside and send debris cascading onto a key highway. With a wry smile, John said he had an interesting story about these demolition munitions. During his tour in command, the brigade had been relocated from one position to another just a few miles away. That made it necessary for John to adapt his plans to the differences in terrain. He discovered there was no sensible way to employ ADMs in the new location. He sent his plan for defending his portion of the gap without use of ADMs up the chain of command. It quickly came back disapproved. His superiors said the ADMs simply had to be included. Argue as he might, John found there was no way he could turn them in or just hold them in reserve. He had to find the least worst way to incorporate ADMs into his plan. That left him the dilemma of what he would actually do in the event of war. It was clear the purpose of these weapons was more for deterrence than for fighting.

That discussion prompted me to ask about the ADMs assigned to my command, and this brought me back to Brenner Pass. It turned out our war plans employed ADMs to destroy concrete pylons about 150 feet high that underpinned the mountainous highway coming through the Brenner. The briefer showed me pictures of the road literally clinging to the mountainside with the support of many of these pylons. In the photos they stood out as narrow, stark white streaks against the background of the gray mountainside and looked very vulnerable. I asked whether charges of conventional explosives could not readily topple them. A stunned silence followed. It was clear this had not even been considered. The fact that we had nuclear weapons that would do the job more assuredly than any other option was enough. There were no calculations to compare not only the effectiveness of the two kinds of explosives but also their ancillary effects, like radioactive fallout, fires, and electromagnetic interference. Getting the road closed and making use of these weapons, not the total consequences, were what mattered.

I did not attempt to take these ADMs out of the war plans. It was not worth the probable arguments. I just assumed I would not use them if war came.

It would be out of character for the United States to initiate the use of nuclear weapons today despite our having done so on two occasions in 1945. We still remain the only nation to have used these weapons. President Harry Truman made that fateful decision at the end of an era when we thought our existence as a society was at stake. The subsequent Cold War era was another in which we thought we were again at such risk.

The post–Cold War era, however, cannot be so characterized. The prospect of our coming under another deadly threat is sufficiently distant that if we forsake the first use of nuclear weapons, doing so will not jeopardize our security. This includes our pledge in 1952 to use nuclear weapons in aid of allies being overwhelmed by a conventional assault. With the end of the Cold War, we have already put additional distance between ourselves and this nuclear guarantee by emphasizing that any use of nuclear weapons on behalf of allies would be a "last resort."[1]

The next step would be to renounce the pledge altogether, but this immediately becomes an emotionally charged issue. There are arguments that Germany would then be driven to acquire its own nuclear weapons; that NATO's very fabric would be rent; and that the United States would be seen as an unreliable ally. It is important to point out that our guaranteed response is to a *conventional* attack, not to a nuclear one. There has always been a question as to whether we would honor this pledge. As noted earlier, Henry Kissinger cautioned the allies not to count on us. Charles de Gaulle felt the same way and said, "No one in the world, and in particular no one in America, can say whether or where or how or to what extent American nuclear weapons would be used to defend Europe."[2]

Today, there is not the slightest prospect of our being called upon to honor this commitment. The countries of the defunct Warsaw Pact, former Soviet allies, are now a buffer between Russia and Western Europe. The Soviet military, once perceived as invincible, has withered to the point of defeat in Afghanistan and Chechnya. Even if Russia resuscitates and grows belligerent again, there is no reason to believe conventional defenses could not defeat any conventional assault it might launch. Russia retained only 49 percent of the Soviet Union's population and 60 percent of its GDP, which has fallen dramatically since. Combined, the United States, Canada, and their European allies have somewhere between ten and fifteen times Russia's GDP today, and more than four times the population; current NATO states will be well ahead economically for a very long time. If Russia does close the gap, NATO would only need to calibrate its conventional force levels to the size and shape of whatever conventional threat reemerges. Whether we and our allies choose to afford the appropriate level of conventional forces is, of course, open to question. Continuing to rely on a nuclear threat would make maintaining adequate conventional forces less likely. Where the European allies, the Germans in particular, do need a U.S. pledge of nuclear support is in the event of nuclear attack. There is no thought of our walking away from that commitment, and I suggest later in this chapter that we would do well to expand that.

This does not mean that our canceling the U.S. nuclear guarantee against conventional attack would be accepted readily. Our European allies usually balk at any change to NATO that they interpret as another step toward U.S. disengagement; but the benefits of our downgrading the utility of these weapons, rather than emphasizing their importance by advertising them in a pledge to use them, outweighs such concern. If Germany one day decides to acquire nuclear weapons, it will do so because it decides its place in the world demands that, not because it does not have our guarantee against a conventional assault on German territory.

If we do not maintain our nuclear pledge to current allies, we certainly would not extend one to any East European states brought into NATO. The East Europeans must surely desire a nuclear umbrella, but the problems with our extending one would be significant. We have always rationalized that in defending NATO our nuclear attacks could be limited to targets in Eastern Europe, meaning any response would most likely be on Western Europe, not the United States. If NATO were expanded eastward, it would find itself on the doorstep of Russia (assuming it reabsorbs Belarus and Ukraine), and thus any nuclear attack would have to be aimed at the Russian homeland. Any retaliation, then, would most likely fall against the United States, and exposing the United States to nuclear retaliation in defending Eastern Europe is more commitment than we should, or will, undertake.

If we were to withdraw our nuclear guarantee in Europe, a strong case could be made for doing the same in Asia. It could be argued, however, that this would enhance China's status in the region, but there is a reasonable probability we could defend South Korea, Taiwan, and Japan from Chinese attacks with conventional forces. We have done it once in Korea; Taiwan and Japan are more readily defensible because they are islands. Conventional defenses would be preferable since China has an intercontinental ballistic missile capability that exceeds our point of self-deterrence.

The strongest argument against a pledge of no first-use is that there are benefits from a posture of calculated ambiguity. The *implied* threat of nuclear attack might be just what it takes to deter some would-be aggressor.

As already suggested in the context of deterring chemical or biological weapons attacks, no such aggressor could afford to assume we meant what we said if we pledged no first-use. At the same time, however, by reserving our right to first-use to protect our interests we directly undermine our efforts to deny others the right to obtain nuclear weapons. Thus, there is a difference of perspective between the deterrent value of ambiguity and the inconsistency created by maintaining that ambiguity as related to our efforts to prevent proliferation. The point here is that the United States making an across-the-board pledge of no first-use could encourage others to do the same.

The United States could first attempt to get Russia and China to agree to bilateral statements of policy renouncing first-use. These would not require extensive negotiation and ratification by the U.S. Senate, as with a treaty. We could also encourage Pakistan and India to develop a similar bilateral policy statement between themselves. Then we could attempt to expand the NPT, which has grown to include 184 members, with a Treaty of No First-Use (NFU). The obligations of such a treaty would be: to renounce the first-use of nuclear weapons; to agree to share intelligence on nations or groups seeking to acquire or use nuclear weapons; and to endorse making any nuclear use a crime against humanity. Since 179 of the 184 NPT signatories are nonnuclear powers, they should have little reason to balk at agreeing not to use them first. A few might be concerned with the possibility of having to condemn a close ally that employed a nuclear weapon, but in signing the treaty they would be agreeing only to a generalized case not pointed at anyone in particular.

Five members of the NPT are acknowledged nuclear powers. Of them, Russia might hold out for a while before joining an NFU (in 1993, Russia withdrew a long-standing unilateral pledge of no first-use out of concern that it might need tactical nuclear weapons to supplement the declining capabilities of its conventional forces). France and Britain might also balk while becoming accustomed to the withdrawal of our nuclear guarantee, but they view themselves as too responsible in the eyes of the international community to hold out for long. China has consistently pledged no first-use and could well join.

Of the handful of nations that are not members of the NPT, three are potential nuclear powers: Israel, India, and Pakistan. On one hand, they might resist joining, because the purpose of their having a nuclear potential is to deter, by threatening first-use, an overwhelming conventional attack on their homelands. India, Pakistan, and Israel thus threaten China, India, and a combined Arab force, respectively. On the other hand, joining the NFU would solve a problem: They are not able to join the NPT because they will not renounce their nuclear potential, and the NPT signatory members will not admit them as additional acknowledged nuclear states. Thus, they appear likely to float as pariahs outside the arms control community indefinitely. That may not appear important to them today, but with the arms control community now encompassing 184 nations, it will be. By joining the NFU, these three would at least gain some status within the community.

A prerequisite for obtaining the agreement of most nonnuclear nations to an NFU would be evidence that the declared nuclear powers were serious about reducing numbers of nuclear weapons as a prelude to eliminating them entirely. The best evidence we could produce would be a vigorous program of strategic escrow by the United States and Russia. With that moving along well, negotiations for a Treaty of No First-Use could be done concurrently with the Phase 2 negotiations for carrying the strategic escrow program to all nuclear powers and to numbers of warheads in the low hundreds.

In any event, an NFU need not have the signatures of even every nuclear power, let alone every nation, to be a valuable step. Those who did not sign would immediately identify themselves as suspects to be watched closely. Even more important, this treaty would be part of shifting our focus from U.S.-Russian nuclear relations to the more probable reasons these weapons might be unleashed: accidents, unauthorized release, and deliberate decisions by lesser nuclear powers or terrorists. Governments in Washington and Moscow have contained the major nuclear threat over the past fifty years, but it will take an international effort to contain the risks that proliferation would pose. The international consensus behind a Treaty of No First-Use would warn any nation with nuclear weapons to handle them carefully and to not be cavalier about their possible use.

Yet one could hope such a treaty would do even more: It could lead to further agreement to impose sanctions against *any* user of a nuclear weapon or any state that was the base for nuclear terrorists. Sanctions are, after all, an accepted device for controlling international behavior. The United Nations has employed sanctions against Iraq since the end of the Gulf War in 1991 and against Libya since 1992 for its suspected role in an act of terrorism. The United States has also used sanctions to try to curtail nuclear proliferation. Sanctions, however, are controversial: Some nations fear setting a precedent that could later be used against them; others refuse to subordinate their commercial relations to the sanctions; others object that economic sanctions often hurt people more than leaders and countries; and still others point out that sanctions are difficult to terminate. Such concerns would carry less weight, however, if sanctions were used against nuclear aggression rather than against proliferation and terrorism, as they are being used currently. There are other possibilities, but the core list of potential sanctions should include:

- Severance of diplomatic ties.
- Ejection from the United Nations.
- Denying admission of the aggressor's aircraft and ships to territorial airspaces and waters.
- Freezing all assets within reach.
- Indictment of the nation or group and its leaders for perpetrating a crime against humanity, as stipulated in the NFU. This provision would supersede the 1996 opinion of the International Court of Justice that first-use of nuclear weapons can be tolerated in exceptional circumstances. (One would hope that the ongoing efforts to create an International Criminal Court succeed, otherwise we would need to organize another, perhaps temporary, jurisdiction, as has been done for Bosnian and Rwandan war crimes trials.)
- Stopping all economic activity with the aggressor, including the severance of as much electronic and mail communication as possible.
- Secondary sanctions against those who deliberately thwart the primary sanctions.
- The use of conventional military force to enforce air and sea blockades.
- The use of conventional military force to remove the nuclear aggressor's government and capture its leadership.

Nations could be allowed to sign on only to the specific sanctions they could accept and enforce. If there were not too many exceptions, these sanctions would cripple any nation that was subjected to them. Even if only the major powers presented a concerted front, that would still be very intimidating. How diligent the signatory states would be in actually applying the sanctions once invoked is uncertain; it would vary with the particular circumstances. The most important point is whether would-be nuclear aggressors could count on sanctions being sufficiently enforced to be crippling. Each such aggressor would evaluate that prospect differently, but all would see the substantial risk in using nuclear weapons or contaminating devices.

The concern that sanctions would be difficult to terminate could be explicitly addressed in separate treaty provisions that allowed for the following: (1) the capture and trial of the leaders responsible before an International Criminal Court; (2) reparations assessed by the International Criminal Court; and (3) the indefinite installation of inspection and control mechanisms to prevent further development and maintenance of weapons of mass destruction. We will have to wait and see how the UN sanctions against Iraq are terminated, but it is encouraging that Iraq's potential for nuclear proliferation sufficiently alarmed the members of the UN Security Council to justify prolonged and highly pervasive intrusions into Iraq's sovereignty. The NFU would be a logical extension of that reasoning. And one of the most attractive features of such a treaty would be its deterrence of terrorists, who have no territory to threaten. The demonstration of international resolve would be sobering even to fanatics, as would the practical steps of sharing intelligence, threatening states that harbor nuclear terrorists, and promising international prosecution.

Responsibility for organizing a Treaty of No First-Use falls to the United States. It would have to work through an ad hoc process, since procedures for drafting treaties in the UN Conference on Disarmament require unanimity, something that would likely be difficult to obtain within a reasonable period. Ideally, the treaty would be administered by the UN Security Council, but we must keep in mind that it would then be subject to the veto power there, raising a risk that its purpose would be subverted. A three-phase progression thus seems necessary.

First: The United States pledges no first-use and promises unilateral sanctions and possibly military actions in the event of nuclear aggression.

Second: The United States negotiates adherence of as many nations as possible to a formal NFU, to be followed by a separate agreement on sanctions and the subsequent construction of an administrative mechanism for managing both treaty and sanctions. Third: The signatories transfer the treaty and the administrative mechanism to the UN after arranging for exemption from the veto power of the UN Security Council's permanent members.

Embarking on such a course would entail considerable risks. It could lead to involvement in nuclear conflicts to which we were not a party. That is unavoidable because if nuclear weapons are used anywhere the United States would inevitably be the dominant force in bringing the nuclear conflict to a halt and in taking steps to prevent recurrence. Failure on our part to play such a role would make further use likely. A greater risk is that of our being forced to take action against friends like Israel, Pakistan, and India. Such a policy is not politically realistic today, especially in the event of Israel's using a nuclear weapon to defend itself against a conventional assault. After all, if we espouse the use of nuclear weapons to defend our European allies against conventional attacks, we could hardly deny Israel, or anyone else, the same right. Fortunately, the Israelis do not want to resort to nuclear defenses because they would be too vulnerable in the long run. We, however, must first get our own house in order by renouncing first-use and then encouraging all of our friends to understand that: (1) we believe that through diplomacy and conventional military preparedness they can ensure their security; (2) we would help them do that and thus avoid their being placed in a position where resort to nuclear weapons seemed necessary;* and (3) in the event of their employing these weapons we would take the side of the greater interests of humankind—avoiding any use of them. In brief, we should let the world know that we are resolutely opposed to anyone initiating nuclear war. We have long pledged to allies that we would come to their aid

---

*In the case of Pakistan, our ability to help them with their defenses would be limited by existing law, which prohibits the transfer of weapons to them. This law was designed to discourage Pakistan from nuclear proliferation. For all intents and purposes that being a fait accompli, we need to devise some new arrangement that would involve restraint in the Pakistani nuclear program, such as Pakistan's joining the Treaty of No First-Use and the United States supporting legitimate Pakistani needs for conventional defenses.

should they become the victim of nuclear attack. This new formulation would expand that assurance to any victim—a universal guarantee of punishment of nuclear aggression using whatever means is appropriate.

There is, of course, good reason to question whether our unilateral guarantee could be expanded into an NFU supplemented with sanctions and then transferred to the UN. There is also the question whether doing all this would necessarily deter rogue states and terrorists. The probability is not very high. However, it is contradictory to attempt to diminish the importance of a weapon while continuing to rely on it as the primary deterrent. The threat of most nations joining to impose sanctions is one alternative deterrent. It is none too soon to begin organizing it or some other substitute for nuclear retaliation. The Phase 2 strategic escrow negotiations would be a logical forum for doing this. But a move away from deterrence by threat of nuclear retaliation will need to be in place before those negotiations could succeed in taking us to truly low numbers of warheads.

We must convince would-be nuclear aggressors that they cannot benefit from such aggression because the strong international aversion and response to use would more than offset any gains they might anticipate. This would open a new dimension to controlling the nuclear genie— building disincentives to nuclear use, not just constraints on acquisition.

7

DEFENSES

In 1968, I COMMANDED THE GUIDED MISSILE CRUISER *USS Horne*. In July of that year *Horne* joined the war in Vietnam and was stationed all alone just twenty miles off the city of Vinh in North Vietnam. We needed to be close to shore in order to provide coverage with our missiles over land. Our assignment was to shoot down any North Vietnamese aircraft that attempted to interfere with U.S. aircraft operating in that area. Being that close to the coast, we were vulnerable to surprise attacks by enemy aircraft slipping out of air bases and quickly flying out to sea. Our missiles could each shoot down only one enemy aircraft. If the North Vietnamese chose to send a sizable number of aircraft simultaneously, we simply could not fire enough of those missiles before some enemy aircraft would reach us. We were vulnerable to being not only taken by surprise but also overwhelmed because our defensive missile system had been designed to operate as part of a team with four to five other guided-missile ships and well out at sea. Here we were, however, in a different type of war than anticipated, operating singly and dangerously close to the threat. The one hope we had for coping was to put nuclear warheads on our missiles. These could destroy a number of attacking aircraft at once. I debated how we might use these warheads in the event of a massed attack. On the one hand, they were all we had that might do the job; on the other, I did not have authority to use them, and the chance of getting that in time was slim. And for all I knew, detonating just one of them could cloud the area with electromagnetic interference and have unpredictable effects on our fighting capabilities. It was all so problematic that I mentally threw up my hands and set tactical nuclear weapons aside as more of an encumbrance than help.

Understanding that this situation in which *Horne* had been placed was unique, I speculated on whether nuclear warheads would be useful in protecting naval forces well out at sea, like aircraft carriers or amphibious groups or merchant ship convoys. In those circumstances, if nuclear weapons were being used it would be vital that the combined defensive systems on all of the ships be able to defeat 100 percent of any attack. Just one nuclear bomb or missile, if reasonably placed, could wipe out a carrier or the heart of an amphibious group or convoy. The probability of total success if we employed conventional warheads on our defensive missiles, against even a modest attack, was negligible. Nuclear-armed missiles would be the only answer. In my twenty-two years of naval service, however, I had never been involved in a training exercise, or even a discussion, that dealt with the tactics of coordinating the use of nuclear defenses among a number of ships. I wondered how the first nuclear warhead to detonate would affect others that followed within a few minutes and whether we could continue to operate our electronic systems effectively once we commenced firing nuclear weapons. It was clear to me we were unprepared for a war at sea waged with nuclear weapons. It could be chaotic and we could be extremely vulnerable.

Our nuclear strategy over the past fifty-plus years has been unique in that defenses have played almost no role. In conventional warfare, a new offensive measure almost always leads rather quickly to a defensive countermeasure, which in turn leads to another new offensive measure. In the context of nuclear weapons, however, the fact that our point of self-deterrence is very low has interrupted this pattern; defenses are worth building only if they are close to perfect. However, the traditional pendulum of defense-offense-defense is so ingrained that we have assumed defenses would play an important role in nuclear strategy.

As far back as the 1950s, we began spending large sums of money to render our strategic forces less vulnerable to surprise attacks by creating the North American Air Defense System, the Ballistic Missile Early Warning System, and an airborne alert system. In 1972, even though it was clear that any defense against ballistic missiles was well beyond both U.S. and Soviet capabilities, we negotiated the Anti-Ballistic Missile (ABM) Treaty to restrict the defenses each side could build; we then built one of two ABM systems permitted under the ABM treaty itself.

In 1983, President Ronald Reagan was persuaded that new technologies would enable us to construct a virtual umbrella over the entire United States that would make it impervious to ballistic missiles, and so he originated the Strategic Defense Initiative (SDI). After spending $45 billion, we have scaled down this ambition.[1] Those who are most hopeful now look for a nationwide defense against limited numbers of ballistic missiles. Others believe a defensive system that extensive would be exorbitant and that we should settle for defending limited areas. The question is this: How much should we invest in the continuing effort to develop and deploy national defenses against nuclear ballistic missile attacks?

In judging any new military system, we measure the expected capabilities against the threat and ask whether the result is worth the costs. To begin evaluating the threat posed by ballistic missile attack, we can look to the Gulf War of 1991. Twenty-eight U.S. military personnel were killed and ninety-eight wounded at their barracks in Saudi Arabia by one Iraqi SCUD ballistic missile;[2] Israel suffered some forty-one SCUD attacks with the loss of two people to direct hits and a number of others to indirect effects. Thus, there already is a threat from short- and medium-range ballistic missiles; these could carry nuclear warheads. Accordingly, we are developing tactical and theater ballistic missile defense systems to protect our interests and those of our allies overseas. With regard to national defenses for the United States, the threat is not so clear. Currently, only Russia and China have the ability to deliver nuclear weapons to U.S. soil with ballistic missiles. Setting aside a major attack from Russia—and defenses against that would be well beyond any foreseeable capability—there could be small attacks, most likely unauthorized launches, or an accident. There is, then, a limited, definable threat from two existing nuclear powers for which national ballistic missile defenses would be appropriate.

The question is whether other nations will acquire nuclear weapons and the intercontinental ballistic missiles needed to deliver them. It is certainly possible, but an intercontinental ballistic missile is a big step up from short-range ones like the SCUD, and it would require great technical know-how to fit the missile with a highly sophisticated nuclear warhead.

Our intelligence community should therefore have a reasonable chance to predict when an intercontinental nuclear threat from ballistic missiles might materialize. In sum, this second threat for which national ballistic missile defenses could be appropriate is currently problematic and warrants close monitoring.

In estimating the capabilities of new defensive systems that we might develop to counter this combination of existing and potential threats, we are faced with the age-old problem that expectations for new weapons are always overly optimistic. We are already hearing that U.S. defenses against limited attacks by ballistic missiles will be 90 percent effective. Having heard similar forecasts for SDI, we ought to judge this against the recent (and only) evidence of our defensive capabilities. During the Gulf War, we employed Patriot missiles to defend against SCUDs. Estimates of the results range from very modest success to failure to destroy even a single warhead.[3] Patriot enjoyed a good record during testing.*

In any event, shooting down ballistic missiles is a formidable technical challenge, and to expect 90 percent success is being very optimistic; there are numerous ways the attacker can complicate and confuse the defenses. The probability of successful defense will alternatively rise and fall as improvements are made in offense and defense. In my view, estimating more than 60–70 percent success against ballistic missile attack would be extremely risky until we have solid evidence from a program of testing. Realistic tests for any destructive military system are difficult and expensive, especially as to ballistic missile defenses. We must afford the expense, however, and the tests must be as realistic as possible. This is not to say that defensive technologies will not improve—just that a cautious skepticism is warranted after many years of meager results.

When it comes to estimating the costs of defenses, we should be wary of unrealistically low estimates. As with almost all new weapons systems, there will be overruns. The fact that we could spend $45 billion on SDI shows how easy it is for vast sums to disappear with only meager results.

There are also nonmonetary costs, and in the case of ballistic missile defenses these could outweigh the monetary ones: The Russians have threat-

---

*It must be acknowledged that Patriot was designed for defending against aircraft and upgraded to deal with ballistic missiles. Still, it is the only antiballistic missile defense system we had available.

ened to retain more offensive weapons than permitted under START II if we proceed further than they think reasonable with ballistic missile defenses, especially if we break the limitations established in the ABM Treaty. This is a contrived concern, but one typical of the unrealistic calculations that characterized U.S. and Soviet nuclear strategy and led us to excessive numbers of nuclear weapons and exceedingly risky doctrines for their use.

The Russians profess concern that they might be vulnerable to a preemptive, disabling nuclear attack by the United States if we had ballistic missile defenses. In this scenario the first step would be a surprise U.S. attack on the Russian nuclear command-and-control system employing SLBMs, which possess a rather short flight time. While the Russians groped for ways to direct their response, U.S. ICBMs would destroy the bulk of Russia's offensive nuclear forces. Russia's surviving retaliatory capability would then be so small that U.S. ballistic missile defenses could further reduce any retaliation to a level the United States could accept.[4] To defeat this tactic, the Russians would retain larger nuclear forces than permitted under START to make it more difficult for the United States to pull off this complicated sequence of actions.

There are so many fallacious assumptions in this scenario it is difficult to believe rational people accept it. Yet there are Russians as well as Americans who accept it while arguing against our building ballistic missile defenses on the grounds that doing so would compel the Russians to violate START II and perhaps renounce START I. Most fundamentally, this line of argument is fallacious in assuming the United States would accept the risks a preemptive attack on Russia would entail. As already mentioned, the U.S. point of self-deterrence is in the neighborhood of one nuclear detonation on our soil. There is no chance this kind of preemptive scheme would shield the United States from serious retaliation because:

- The probability our intelligence apparatus could locate every element in Russia's command-and-control system so that not even one command post survived to sound the alarm is zero.
- The probability of our attacking Russia's ICBMs with near-perfect success is also zero. In war there is always, to use Clausewitz's terminology, "friction" and "fog." People make mistakes; equipment does not perform up to standards; the enemy responds in unexpected ways; uncontrollable forces like the weather

interfere. In this scenario we assume U.S. ICBMs will be reliable after flying a trajectory over the North Pole, something never done in practice; and that they will land within a few hundred feet of their aim point after traveling 5,000-plus miles. In real life, some would not even get off the ground; some would not reach Russia at all; some would get there but not come close enough to the target to damage it; and some of those arriving at their targets would not detonate. We build redundancy into our war plans for such contingencies, but the probability of covering every error that develops is minuscule.

- The probability that we could destroy the bulk of Russia's SSBNs, land-based mobile ICBMs, and bombers is very low. All are difficult to locate and currently carry 42 percent of Russia's strategic nuclear warheads.[5]
- There is at least some probability that if we had a very capable nationwide ballistic missile defense system the Russians would have one also. Only if they did not would 100 percent of our initial, disabling attack get through. It would be painful for the Russians to afford such defenses today, but if they believed their national survival appeared to be at stake they might make the necessary sacrifices.

We can make some approximate calculations:

- If Russia's nuclear forces were at a level of 3,000 warheads and we assume (unrealistically, but to present an extreme case) that we could preemptively destroy 90 percent of the immobile weapons and 50 percent of the mobile ones; that our ballistic missile defenses were 70 percent effective; and that 10 percent of Russia's weapons failed due to friction, the number of Russian warheads that would impact the United States would be a clearly unacceptable 539. If we are even less realistic and assume 90 percent effective ballistic missile defenses and 50 percent failures due to friction, the United States would still receive 233 warheads.
- Scaling downward to 1,000 warheads in the Russian arsenal, seventy-eight would survive and penetrate to the United States under the most severe of these assumptions.

- Scaling down even further to 250 warheads, the resulting attack on the United States would be twenty warheads.* It is difficult to imagine that a president could justify initiating a nuclear war that resulted in the loss of even one American city, let alone twenty. What conceivable gain could that president point to that would convince the public it was worth it?

Still, numbers like twenty, or even seventy-seven, can sound like dangerously thin margins that could be eroded by some technological breakthrough. Yet they are not, because neither we nor the Russians would agree to go below 1,000 warheads without taking additional steps to ensure against preemption. For instance, rather than sit by and accept 90 percent vulnerability of fixed ICBMs, we each would shift to submarines and bombers that are considerably less vulnerable; neither side would accept 90 percent attrition of ICBMs and SLBMs to ballistic missile defenses when greater reliance on cruise missiles could bypass such defenses; and each would insist on measures to provide warning of any preemptive effort, such as a program of strategic escrow.

It takes extremely unrealistic assumptions to lower the threat of retaliation to a preemptive attack to a worrisome number, that is, to make traditional deterrence questionable. Because the dynamics of deterrence will change as numbers in the arsenals decline, deterrence by threat can be continued down to very low numbers. We should be pleased that at lower numbers we will be pushed to rely less on pure threat of retaliation and more on passive measures like warning and secure retaliatory forces.

Thus, any scenario that rests on the assumption of a successful U.S. preemptive attack on Russia is simply irrational, and we should not base national defense decisionmaking on such a premise. Nor should we encourage the Russians to believe it by pandering to an argument based on it. Moreover, there are costs for endorsing the preemptive thesis. One is that our nuclear arsenal became inflated, in part, by our concern over the so-called window of vulnerability. As far back as the 1950s, General Curtis LeMay used what, in retrospect, was a badly flawed RAND analysis to justify more strategic bombers to offset their supposed vulnerability. Similarly, this con-

---

*The calculations behind these numbers are given in Appendix C.

cern over vulnerability led us to risky precautionary procedures, such as keeping nuclear weapons on high alert and enabling presidents to exercise the nuclear option with only a few minutes' consideration.

Our focus on vulnerability to preemptive attack has also diverted much of our efforts in arms control to issues of lesser importance. In negotiating SALT II, we worried about how many warheads the Soviets might be able to slip surreptitiously onto their very large ICBMs in order to overwhelm us preemptively. The treaty could have fallen apart over whether we could keep track of the number of warheads actually on their ICBMs. Fourteen years later, during the START II negotiations, one of our key objectives was to eliminate all Russian ICBMs capable of carrying more than one warhead to prevent their being able to load up extra warheads for preemptive purposes. We surely could have negotiated some provision of greater value than that of reducing a nonexistent threat.

An insidious cost of our preoccupation with preemption is that it perpetuates the notion that the United States and Russia are doomed to an adversarial relationship. We did fight the long Cold War with the Soviet Union, but we once fought hot wars with Germany and Japan, who now are allies. Why assume Russia cannot be encouraged into a stable, responsible nuclear posture like Britain and France? Why assume a relationship of tension and not of friendship? There is nothing to lose by exploring this, as we need not be naive and take risks in the process.

The idea of successful preemption has also fostered the false impression that the ABM Treaty is vital to our security. It is time to recognize that this treaty has had its day. In 1972, we and the Soviets understood that ballistic missile defenses were not then achievable. Engaged in an expensive race for more nuclear weapons, each was eager to avoid another costly and fruitless competition, hence the ABM Treaty, which limited defensive systems. Since the Russians cannot afford a race for defenses today, the restraints this treaty imposes are no longer necessary. The Russians might, as noted above, be forced to follow along with us in building defenses, but the pace of ballistic missile defense research and development is our option. It was an option we could easily forego while focusing on a bilateral nuclear relationship and the possibility of very large attacks. We could just assume these weapons were self-deterring or that no defenses could stop a massive attack.

Given the potential for additional hostile nuclear powers, we must look at the defensive option differently. The threat of nuclear attack could be more real—but also small enough that defenses could make a difference. Ballistic missile defenses deserve to be judged on the same basis as tactical and theater defenses, that is, on costs, capabilities, and threats, not on whether they would make Russia vulnerable to a preemptive attack or scuttle the ABM Treaty.

This is not to suggest the Russians might not feel vulnerable should we build defenses. They could decide to retain larger nuclear forces or even break START I and START II. That would be unfortunate but not necessarily a serious blow. Because the logic of Russia's potential vulnerability to our defenses will not hold up, the Russian position would be an expression of their frustration at having become a second-tier power for the time being. Since they remain a superpower in the nuclear arena only, there is great temptation to hold onto every shred of prestige. Maintaining excessive numbers of nuclear weapons for the purpose of political prestige, however, will inevitably conflict with other political objectives and with their economic position. For instance, when President Yeltsin proposed a force level of 2,000–2,500 warheads during the START II negotiations in 1993, he presumably wanted the least expensive solution for Russia. He must also have been aware of outside pressures from a number of nonnuclear NPT signatory nations for lower numbers. And should Russia falter on START II, it would jeopardize a wide range of U.S. support. The trend to lower numbers is firmly set, its importance too well understood, for it to falter for long thanks to an irrational premise.

To help avoid any delay in the nuclear arms reduction process, we could take actions to ease the impact of our moves. For example:

- Stress the U.S. commitment to reach about 250 warheads. There is a commonly accepted view that defenses make low numbers dangerous because they may defeat any small retaliation, but that assumes 100 percent successful defense. Even against small attacks, that is not realistic. Instead, maintaining a low number of warheads is reassuring, as it would show a lack of interest in a preemptive policy.
- Emphasize a U.S. pledge of no first-use.
- Renew the offer President Reagan made in 1985 to share research on defenses. We could invite capable Russian scientists to work here, at least to the point that Russia would have warning if a

possible danger to them developed. If the Russians understood that the best we could hope for was to defeat small attacks, as would very likely be the case, they would see that the strategic balance would not be upset.

In making our decisions on national ballistic missile defenses, we must also address the costs of defending against less sophisticated means of nuclear attack through unconventional means of delivery, such as:

- A cruise missile attack at a U.S. coastal city from a merchant ship;
- A bomb smuggled aboard a ship into a U.S. port;
- A bomb placed on a national airliner with permission to fly into the United States;
- A sneak intrusion by a relatively small aircraft with a modest nuclear bomb; and
- A bomb concealed inside a truck and smuggled across the Mexican or Canadian border.

Surreptitious nuclear attacks on such a limited basis would not threaten U.S. society as a whole but could present grim local problems to say the least. A key line of defense is found in the U.S. intelligence community's ability to detect the plans to infiltrate the weapons. This would range from identifying people acquiring materials for the manufacture of weapons to uncovering arrangements to delivering them. While Director of Central Intelligence, I saw us successfully infiltrate a terrorist group, learn from the inside exactly what was planned, and then thwart it. Unfortunately, the odds of such successes are not high.

A more likely scenario is that we must be ready to physically prevent smuggling of nuclear explosives. That is a formidable challenge. Just being able to conduct surveillance of U.S. borders for this purpose would require great resources and development of new techniques of detection, such as more sensitive sensing devices for radioactivity. Any system of thorough inspection could involve inordinate delays in routine travel and restrict the right of individuals to free movement. Our public might tolerate the required intrusiveness, but perhaps only if there were obvious reason to do so, such as a nuclear incident. Fortunately, the current need for border surveillance is low, but we cannot wait until a crisis is upon us to make plans, train people, and develop equipment. We must look at it as a military contingency plan. FEMA, the Department of Energy, and the Department of Defense are reportedly working in this direction. We need to ensure that this work is pursued vigorously, as with ballistic missile defenses, and add these costs to those of building defense systems. One without the other is illogical.

There is another nonmonetary cost: Rogue states and terrorists might acquire U.S. defensive technologies. Yet if we were to share them with the Russians and our allies, there would be limited hope for preventing others from obtaining them. Any attempt to keep this knowledge exclusive would be seen as nuclear hegemony and undermine our efforts for international cooperation to prevent the spread or use of nuclear weapons. The proliferation of ballistic missile defenses will not be an immediate problem, however. A few nations with special needs and with high-technological capabilities like Israel, South Korea, Taiwan, and Japan may develop them, but for most they will not be easy to build but will be expensive, technologically complex, difficult to operate, and subject to friction. We have the choice of accepting the gradual proliferation of ballistic missile defenses or foregoing them.

Finally, we have to consider another cost: the impact that building strategic defenses would have on the other nuclear powers:

- China has already objected to the possibility of our giving ballistic missile defense technologies to Taiwan and Japan. It professes that placing such defenses in those countries could blunt the Chinese nuclear threat, allowing them to be more aggressive toward China. Their concern, however, does not have merit. Possessing about 500 nuclear warheads, China could easily overwhelm any Japanese or Taiwanese defenses. In addition, these countries pose no military threat to China. The unspoken concern is that China could not threaten the United States with its limited intercontinental force if we possess even modest defenses. They did just that in 1996 during a crisis between them and the Taiwanese when they pointedly and publicly reminded us that their ICBMs could reach Los Angeles. The obvious implication was that we should be wary of intervening on the side of Taiwan. It will, then, be difficult to assuage the Chinese, but our selfish interest in not being

vulnerable and our interest in deterring China—or anyone—from using nuclear blackmail dictate that we ignore this complaint.
- The British and the French profess to fear that if Russia were to have a defensive system, it might feel free to attack them. Combined, France and Britain possess approximately 750 nuclear warheads. Russia is a long way from building defenses that could blunt those retaliatory capabilities. Again, we have no reason not to proceed as these allies will weather any tempest they create.

Foregoing national defenses against ballistic missile attack is not a serious option. The only question is one of pace. We have been investing in their development for more than thirty years. In 1965, Secretary of Defense Robert S. McNamara did not believe national defenses were warranted, yet he was forced by domestic political pressures to endorse and fund a system designed to blunt small attacks. This should remind us that defenses are inherently attractive since they focus on protection rather than destruction. And the difference between having limited defenses that could shoot down an errant or deliberate attack of just a few missiles and not having one and seeing a nuclear weapon detonate on, say, New York or Washington, would be enormous. Moreover, the work we are doing to develop theater ballistic missile defenses is bound to raise the temptation to expand them to serve national purposes. It is never easy to curtail a new military technology that promises substantially improved military capabilities. That is what keeps the warfare pendulum of offense-defense-offense swinging. That pendulum has been on the side of the offense in nuclear strategy for a long time; that it will stay there indefinitely is unlikely.

There is, then, a definite role for national defenses in promoting nuclear stability. For those who want to see the world reduce to zero nuclear weapons, national defenses against very small attacks would be reassuring. For those who prefer to see the world with very limited numbers of nuclear weapons, national defenses will help move us away from the risks that go with threatening devastating retaliation. There is no reason for the United States not to come out unequivocally in favor of national defenses against both ballistic missiles and other forms of attacks with nuclear weapons. It certainly would be foolish not to do so because of an irrational theory about Russian vulnerability to a U.S. preemptive attack. But it is also a time for us to have the humility to recognize the delicacy of Russia's position. No wonder they believe this irrational business about preemptive attacks! We must be persuaded that defenses are needed urgently before we risk turning the cooperative relationship with Russia on nuclear arms reductions into an adversarial one. We need not slow down research, even if that should break the ABM Treaty, because any threat that research poses is distant; considering the record of the past forty years, it is very difficult to stop research in this particular field.

The overarching point is that integrating national defenses with sharply reduced numbers of offensive nuclear weapons should be seen as an important opportunity to further nuclear stability.

8

A NEW VISION

IN MARCH 1977, JUST A WEEK AFTER BECOMING Director of Central Intelligence, I attended my first meeting of the National Security Council (NSC) in the cabinet room of the White House. The topic was forthcoming nuclear arms negotiations with the Soviet Union. President Gerald Ford had left recently inaugurated President Jimmy Carter a nearly completed agreement, which we had been negotiating with the Soviet Union since November 1972. President Carter now opened this meeting by stating he thought we could make much larger reductions than those in the draft agreement. To my amazement, he then briefed us on what he intended to propose to the Soviets. Even though he had been in office only two months, he knew as much about the topic as anyone in the room. Unfortunately, within a few weeks Secretary General Leonid Brezhnev had rejected President Carter's ambitious proposal out of hand. That sent us back to the drawing board and into the painstaking process of negotiating terms that would likely split differences between the Ford and Carter proposals.

It was painstaking to get agreement from all of the parties involved: the heads of the Arms Control and Disarmament Agency and the Departments of State, Defense, and Justice; myself; and, of course, the president. And to maneuver through the Byzantine bureaucracy in Moscow was not any easier. Sometimes Secretary of State Cyrus Vance would travel to Moscow; sometimes he would deal with Soviet ambassador Anatoly Dobrynin in Washington; other times he would leave it to a negotiating team permanently in Geneva. Whenever we thought we had some detail nailed down, a new wrinkle would develop somewhere in the Soviet system. After a year and a half we were making progress toward what was to be the Strategic Arms Limitation Treaty II (SALT II). Then, in December 1978, during discussions in Moscow, Cy Vance ran into several roadblocks with the Soviets that he could not resolve. He tossed them back to the NSC with his recommendations for adjustments we might make.

One of these was of key importance to my responsibility for ensuring that our intelligence mechanism could verify whatever terms were negotiated in the treaty. I believed we needed a provision prohibiting the Soviets from coding the telemetry signals from ICBMs that they test fired. Telemetry is the means by which performance data generated inside a test missile are signaled back to the launchpad so the engineers can monitor the missile's performance. We could intercept those signals and use the data to check on several provisions of the draft treaty (e.g., a missile's total carrying capacity). The Soviets had told Cy they would not include a prohibition against the coding of telemetry in the treaty; instead they would give us oral assurances. In the atmosphere of the Cold War it was difficult to accept such a promise; this would have been particularly troubling to the U.S. Senate, which had to ratify any treaty we negotiated.

Cy was pressing for immediate instructions. We needed a meeting of the NSC, but President Carter was ill and in Plains, Georgia. Instead, there was a meeting that evening in Zbigniew Brzezinski's office. His office, with its high ceilings and its eight-foot windows, which allowed one to look out onto the front lawn of the White House, normally seemed spacious and airy. But with every interested department and agency represented it was uncomfortably crowded, and most of us were juggling papers in our laps. We all hoped to avoid having to disturb the ill president to resolve any differences among us.

But there was this stumbling block of whether to insist on a provision against the coding of telemetry. I knew how much President Carter wanted this treaty. But I also knew that if I could not give the senators a firm assurance we could verify every provision precisely, it might fail ratification. Yet it was clear to me that all this anxiety over coding telemetry was a tempest in a teapot. So what if the Soviets cheated and added some warheads? They had more than 40,000 of them already. A few more would hardly be noticeable. However, it was not my responsibility to judge the political and military importance of Soviet cheating but to certify whether we could catch them if they did. I believed we could do that only if there was no coding of telemetry.

I held to my position, which forced a phone call to the president. When Zbig got through to the Carter home in Plains, he was told the president had been sedated and was asleep. Zbig persisted, and as we waited he turned on a speaker on his desk so everyone could hear the president. When a groggy Jimmy Carter came on the line he must have expressed some considerable displeasure, because Zbig quickly turned off the speaker. We all listened to Zbig explain my position and the alternative of accepting oral assurances from the Soviets. The president decided to accept oral assurances. What really was at stake was persuading senators to ratify the treaty, and the president obviously understood our chances better than I did. It was clear nobody was concerned with the possibility of actual cheating.

Still, this issue of telemetry was consuming an inordinate amount of time of a number of the top leaders of our government; it was also threatening the impending treaty. Thus, the importance we had attached to nuclear parity was coming close to thwarting a historic effort at arms control. And given the large numbers of nuclear weapons on each side, that simply did not make any sense. For the next nine months, I worked diligently to persuade senators that we could check on the Soviets as closely as was necessary. It looked as though reason would prevail and that telemetry would not be a roadblock to ratification.

The Soviets invaded Afghanistan on December 25, 1979, and SALT II suddenly came apart at the seams.

THE PROCESS OF ARMS CONTROL has been painfully slow, often because it was diverted onto issues of little substance. This is unlikely to change—witness that the very best prospect from the Clinton-Yeltsin summit of 1997 is that the year 2010 will see the United States and Russia still with 2,000–2,500 warheads each. There are valid reasons why we should not accept such a dilatory program.

First, we should appreciate how fortunate we are that the more bizarre of our policies during the Cold War (e.g., sitting on hair-trigger alert with thousands of nuclear warheads) did not lead to nuclear war. Given the intensity of the superpower confrontation then, this is nothing less than miraculous. There are some people, however, who argue just the opposite, that is, because nuclear weapons are excessively powerful the risks of employing them are obvious and over time they will become superfluous.

This thesis overlooks the fact that leaders of responsible nations will insist on playing an active role in shaping policy toward weapons of this magnitude—and that leaders of irresponsible nations may not worry enough about the consequences of using them. Thus, we cannot escape the necessity of managing the residue of our Cold War nuclear policies.

Beyond this general concern, we must recognize how unpredictable Russia and China are today. They could become democratic and stable or autocratic and lawless; aggressive and predatory or cooperative and observant of international laws and commitments. It is very much in our interest to see to it that nuclear weapons play as small a role as possible during these transformations. For instance, we would not want to see Russia and China adopt the U.S. policy of nuclear response to conventional attack. And we would not want to see either country rely so heavily on nuclear forces as to make it difficult to agree to further reductions. Getting these weapons off the table as soon as possible is our best precaution.

We must also limit the risk of proliferation. In the early 1990s, we saw all too clearly how far Iraq and North Korea had moved in this direction. Given that fissionable materials and nuclear technology are increasingly available, we need to focus considerable attention on uncovering and defeating efforts to acquire nuclear capabilities.

Unfortunately, the Cold War vision for nuclear stability has not given us a rationale for where we want to go in terms of numbers of nuclear weapons. This is the case despite the fact that the most significant accomplishment of the arms control process has been to challenge the thesis that more is always better, thereby setting us on the path to reduced numbers. The implicit assumption has been that after substantially reducing numbers of warheads, perhaps to the low hundreds, we would somehow jump to zero. Every U.S. president during the nuclear era has stated an explicit preference for zero, and today there is increasing attention to making that our objective. National and international study groups with prestigious personages, like former secretaries of defense, Nobel Peace Prize recipients, ambassadors, admirals, generals, and international figures from many other disciplines have concluded that going to zero is preferable to trying to live with small numbers. This view that nuclear disarmament is the best solution, then, deserves careful consideration. Is it feasible? Is it desirable?

Nuclear disarmament is not feasible in the foreseeable future because no one knows how to take the last few steps to zero warheads without risking that one of the nuclear powers would clandestinely retain a few. Going to zero and staying there demands a regime for verification and control light-years beyond anything we have in place today. It would include virtually every country in the world; all civil and military uses of nuclear energy; and a detailed accounting of all existing weapons, weapons components, means of production, and stocks of fissile materials. The overall commitment of resources would be immense. There must also be a mechanism to deal with violators, which would exceed any authority the world has yet granted to international organizations. The extent of this challenge is exemplified by the fact that although the UN has accorded itself unprecedented intrusion into the sovereignty of Iraq, it has been unable to certify that it has located all of that country's facilities for producing weapons of mass destruction. Even advocates of nuclear disarmament acknowledge it is decades away and will require fundamental changes in the relations of nations.

These same advocates, however, point to the amazing progress over the past several decades with respect to intrusive inspections and infringement into sovereignties. They argue this is likely to accelerate with experience and that only by declaring a goal of zero will we impress upon ourselves, and the world, the notion that nuclear weapons are not useful. One of the most prestigious of these advocates, the Canberra Commission on the Elimination of Nuclear Weapons, which was convened in 1995–1996 by the Australian government, stated the case for zero thus: "Nuclear weapons are held by a handful of states which insist that these weapons provide unique security benefits, and yet reserve uniquely to themselves the right to own them. This situation is highly discriminatory and thus unstable; it cannot be sustained. The possession of nuclear weapons by any state is a constant stimulus to other states to acquire them."[1]

It is rather logical to conclude that if a few nations have nuclear weapons and most do not, some nonnuclear nations would try to get them. If nuclear weapons are useful for some, they almost certainly must be for others also. Going to zero would eliminate that element of instability—but it would incite another: If no one ostensibly possesses nuclear weapons, the potential leverage that stems from being the only one in the world with them would appear to be enormous. One day we must decide whether chances of proliferation are greater if no one has nuclear weapons or if a few do. This is not a matter that begs for immediate resolution.

Should we, then, establish nuclear disarmament as the cornerstone of our nuclear policy? One argument for doing so is a provision in the NPT committing us to move ultimately to nuclear disarmament. Some of the nonnuclear signatories to the NPT already are looking for ways to hold U.S. and Russian feet to the fire. These nations could, for instance, refuse to cooperate in sensible measures to reduce nuclear risks, like agreeing to a Treaty of No First-Use. Our failure to advocate zero, then, could impede international cooperation to forestall the use of nuclear weapons. But this must be weighed against the disadvantage on the domestic side. Getting safely to zero is too distant and problematic an objective to generate public enthusiasm for having that as our goal. We would more likely obtain public and congressional support if the objective were more limited and achievable. We need not, however, walk away from the commitment we have made under the NPT to work toward the elimination of nuclear weapons. We would emphasize it primarily in the international arena, and only to the extent needed to obtain international cooperation on such matters as expanding the NPT into a Treaty of No First-Use. On the domestic side we would stress more clearly defined objectives, such as the strategic escrow program.

When we reach the point at which the nuclear powers choose whether to continue from low numbers to zero, the deciding factor will be their level of confidence in thereafter preventing anyone from acquiring nuclear weapons. If they are very confident, going to zero would be the preferable option. It would be equivalent to disinventing nuclear weapons and would eliminate any concern that someone might employ one. It is precisely this hope that propels advocates of disarmament. However, having total confidence in eliminating proliferation is unlikely. Thus, one day we must compare the risks at zero with the risks inherent in a new vision based on strategic escrow, a Treaty of No First-Use supplemented with sanctions, and modest defenses.

The first component of the vision of nuclear stability, a program of strategic escrow, would establish a clear rationale for an endpoint: taking all nuclear powers below the points of non-recovery of the United States, Russia, and China. If, for instance, after additional study, 250 warheads is fixed as our best estimate of the points of non-recovery for these larger countries, our target for each nation's maximum inventory might be 200. That would have to be the absolute total in each arsenal, lest reserves be employed to get back above the points of non-recovery. It has been our practice to hold reserves of warheads for failures of one sort or another and for maintenance. Such concerns are predicated on Cold War requirements for precise amounts of damage under strategies to win wars, whereas in more realistic MIT-type strategies eliminating precise numbers of targets is not essential. After getting to maximums of 200, we would want to place all of those warheads in escrow. The probability of surprise attack would disappear. The final objective would be to place all warheads in escrow under international observation, thus ensuring that an alarm would be sounded if any nuclear power withdrew warheads to remount them on delivery vehicles. That would take us very close to nuclear disarmament. At the same time, if some rogue state surreptitiously acquired nuclear weapons, sufficient weapons could be taken from escrow to deter blackmail or use.

The proposed Treaty of No First-Use, the second element of the new vision, would move us away from relying on the threat of nuclear retaliation as the road to deterrence. Sharing intelligence would, one hopes, stimulate international action to prevent proliferation. An accompanying threat of international sanctions of various sorts would also be a powerful disincentive to proliferation. And making any use of nuclear weapons a crime against humanity should help dispel any ideas that these weapons are useful. Historically, there has been an unwillingness on the part of nuclear powers to press their nuclear advantage, even against nonnuclear powers. For example, from 1950 to 1953 the United States fought a war in Korea without winning but did not resort to nuclear weapons; in 1962, the United States and the Soviet Union carefully avoided pushing the Cuban missile crisis to the point of nuclear explosion; from 1965 to 1972, the United States fought and lost in Vietnam without employing nuclear weapons; from 1979 to 1989, the Soviet Union fought and lost in Afghanistan without using nuclear weapons; and in 1991, when the United States and its nuclear-armed allies, Britain and France, fought Iraq, the senior U.S. military officer discarded the idea of using nuclear weapons because he found it tactically unsound. This is not to say that there were not serious discussions about our using nuclear capabilities in some of these situations. Rather, it tells us that when consideration of doing so reached presidents, or those close to them, the idea was always rejected.

Why such restraint? First, there always looms the magnitude of retalia-tion, that is, self-deterrence. Second, there has long been an undercurrent of concern, going back to President Eisenhower's shock at finding that his nuclear war plan, if executed, would have killed 175 million people, over the amount of damage nuclear weapons would do to an opponent. Third, it seems impossible to use nuclear weapons without unwanted side ef-fects, for example, damages to one's own territory or forces; blast, heat, and radiation effects extending past an actual target; and disruption of food and water supplies and essential services such as medical, fire fight-ing, and shelter. The fourth reason for such restraint is that we do not want the United States to be accused of being Carthage's Rome or of grossly violating the Geneva Convention against attacking innocent civil-ians. If those are restraints, the utility of nuclear weapons is limited to the most dire circumstances. It is because of this that we have never been able to develop plans for the use of nuclear weapons that would ensure any real benefit (and that is my opinion, based on what I have seen of those plans over the years). It is easy to conclude, then, that a combination of tactical limitations and moral implications makes nuclear weapons even less usable than dum-dum bullets, poison gas, and biological weapons, all of which have been outlawed. Nuclear weapons cannot be the solution to anyone's problems.

We must also use treaties and sanctions to persuade others of the limited value of these weapons. That would take us much closer to a permanent solution than the traditional programs of denial and threat. Admittedly, there will be nations so mesmerized by the power of nuclear weapons that it will be difficult to persuade them. And it would be difficult to make a case persuasively against use when a country with nuclear capability has its back absolutely against the wall in a conventional war or is seeking redress for a perceived grievous wrong, like an attack with biological weapons. Still, U.S. leadership should be able to persuade nations that the effect of unleashing the nuclear genie would be a disaster for the human race.

The third element of the new vision, modest defenses when feasible, is only likely to be meaningful against limited nuclear attacks. Still, it would be one more step away from our nearly exclusive reliance on the threat of nuclear retaliation to deter. Because it has been difficult to define just what level of threat it takes to deter, a strategy of retaliation has inflated requirements for numbers of nuclear weapons. The longer we remain wedded to that policy, the longer it will take to progress downward in numbers. Moreover, it is unnatural in warfare that defenses play almost no role, and we are reaching the point where we will have to adjust our strategies as defenses progressively improve, but points of self-deterrence are simply too low, and prospective defensive capabilities too limited, for this to be a major change. Still, every step away from exclusive reliance on threatening nuclear retaliation will be all to the good. We should welcome this changing environment for strategic defenses with the confidence that we can find ways to integrate them into a stable nuclear equation as they become progressively more capable.

This new vision encompasses a world with as few nuclear nations as possible, with each nation possessing as few nuclear weapons as possible, and with all of those weapons in supervised escrow, plus the threat of sanctions against first-use and modest defenses as a backup against limited attack. This vision is at least competitive with the idea of nuclear disarmament. As noted earlier, the final decision will hinge on our confidence in meeting the exacting demands of nuclear disarmament—intrusive inspections and controls. In the meantime, the new vision deals clearly with our three principal concerns with nuclear weapons:

- First, at the high end of the "risk scale," the U.S.-Russian nuclear relationship could possibly degenerate into a war that no side can hope to win. But with overall numbers low and with surprise attacks unlikely thanks to strategic escrow, there would be a good chance of averting the kinds of misunderstandings and miscalculations that could lead to such a catastrophe.
- Second, there is the lesser danger that small nuclear wars will erupt, perhaps involving the United States, perhaps not. The intimidating effect of potential sanctions would make nuclear aggression unrewarding and should help to deter this.
- Third, there is the threat of nuclear terrorism. Building an international consensus in a Treaty of No First-Use that nuclear war must be prevented would be one measure to meet the threat. If faced with international sharing of intelligence, sanctions against nations that harbor nuclear terrorists, and a law making nuclear use a crime against humanity, terrorists would have to appreciate the extent of opposition they would encounter.

None of these is a certain solution, of course. Whatever vision we endorse, however, must attempt to address all of these concerns. The important point is not that this new vision is the only vision or that every piece of this vision must be adopted at once. What we want to appreciate is that the ending of the Cold War has provided an opportunity to step back and evaluate nuclear policy more objectively. Such a review will show that the manmade nuclear weapon contains such immense destructive power that it is no longer useful. That conclusion rests on both a sense of morality and a pragmatic evaluation of benefits; it will not necessarily be shared by all nations of the world. Some will estimate net benefits differently. Some will have quite different concepts of morality. It is our responsibility to persuade such nations that from a pragmatic standpoint they will never gain from using nuclear weapons, that is, to ensure they understand the costs will be so high that they cannot benefit by resorting to the nuclear option. What we should hope for, however, is that a wider sense of morality and greater concern for humankind will be generated over time, to the point that an unleashing of the nuclear genie is so unlikely that threats of retaliation become unnecessary.

In the best of worlds, we could even hope that an understanding of both the pragmatic and moral impediments to the use of nuclear weapons would gradually apply also to conventional warfare. How many conventional wars have been fought to achieve objectives that simply were not achievable through the use of force? How much of the world's wealth has gone into armaments that were in excess of any legitimate need? Is it too idealistic to hope that an understanding of why nuclear weapons are difficult to employ usefully, and of why we came to spend wildly unnecessary sums on them, will in time be applied to progressively lesser forms of violence, until they are finally removed from the world's agenda?

The United States must shoulder the responsibility of bringing such a vision to the world, in part because it was we who introduced nuclear weapons, but, more importantly, because we are the only nation with the combination of conscience and wherewithal to undertake such a responsibility. After World War II, the United States was in a position to design and implement the Marshall Plan. After the Cold War, we are in a position to lead the world into a plan to cage the nuclear genie. Would that we could put it back in the bottle!

9

RESHAPING DECISIONMAKING

IN JUNE 1979, PRESIDENT CARTER CALLED A MEETING of the National Security Council to decide whether or not to ask Congress to fund the development of the MX ballistic missile system. It was my responsibility as Director of Central Intelligence to open such meetings by presenting relevant intelligence data. It was not my province to suggest what the president should decide, lest that appear to prejudice my appraisal of the facts. There were times, however, that it was very difficult not to get involved in the heart of the discussion. This was one of those instances. What I did was to offer an analysis of what the Soviet response would be if we built the MX and fielded it using the forty-three shelter "racetrack" scheme. This was close to offering an opinion, that is, that the basing plan was bizarre and the MX was unnecessary.

The conclusion in the CIA was that the Soviets would counter our deployment of the MX in some way. We expected their reaction to be similar to what ours would be: Threaten as much of the opponent's military force as possible. We decided they would aim one warhead at each of the forty-three moderately hardened shelters on the racetracks rather than attempt to discern which shelter actually contained the missile. They would have enough warheads under SALT II, which we were then negotiating, to do that. Thus, the effect of creating forty-three shelters for each MX, rather than placing them in standard, vulnerable ICBM silos, would be to invite more nuclear detonations on our soil in the event of nuclear war.

There was no rebuttal to this line of reasoning from those present representing military interests, the secretary of defense and the chair of the

Joint Chiefs of Staff, or from Zbig Brzezinski, who favored the MX. They simply shifted the discussion to whether the president should select a large- or moderate-size version of the missile. My opinion was that the smaller MX was decidedly preferable because we would have the option of making it modestly mobile, and hence less vulnerable, by mounting it on a truck trailer, a railroad car, or an aircraft. What our military clearly wanted was the most powerful counterweight to the even larger ICBMs on the Soviet side. The unspoken argument favoring the larger missile, however, was that nothing less would placate those senators who were wavering on whether to ratify SALT II. It was going to be nip and tuck in garnering the sixty-seven votes necessary for approval. The president had to hook some of the senators who were in doubt, and the MX was the bait.

As the meeting drew to a close, President Carter said, in effect, "As I understand the discussion, everyone agrees we should proceed with the MX and in the larger version." I raised my hand: "Mr. President, it is not my role to comment on policy issues, but your use of 'everyone' included me. I do not agree." Not unexpectedly, this had no effect.

CHANGING THE UNDERLYING PREMISES of our nuclear policies as fundamentally as I have suggested would require dedicated leadership by president and Congress alike. We have aspired in the past to similarly dramatic changes but have always failed. In 1946, we submitted the Acheson-Lilienthal/Baruch plan to the United Nations for international control over nuclear technology, either for weapons or energy, with the end objective being to dispense with nuclear weapons entirely. The Soviet Union thought this was a guise for perpetuating U.S. nuclear hegemony, and the plan was killed almost the moment it was submitted. In 1986, in Reykjavik, Iceland, Ronald Reagan and Mikhail Gorbachev, working without advisers, almost agreed to eliminate either all ballistic missiles (the U.S. proposal) or all strategic nuclear weapons (the Soviet proposal) within ten years. This startling breakthrough foundered on differences over strategic defenses.

The question today is whether these precedents suggest we should proceed cautiously toward similarly revolutionary changes, or, with the end of the Cold War, whether we should hold out for even greater change. In my view, the forces of resistance are sufficiently in retreat that a firm commitment from a president could move us forward aggressively. Moreover, to proceed piecemeal would only play into the hands of those who will seek to slow the process at every stage.

Surprisingly, however, presidents have not played decisive roles in deciding numbers of nuclear weapons or plans for targeting them, although they certainly knew that the numbers in our arsenal and the amount of damage designed into our war plans were excessive. We can surmise a number of reasons for their reluctance to grapple directly with these wasteful and risky practices. One is that mastering nuclear terminology and technology is time consuming. It also requires perseverance, because military officers are always reluctant to involve civilians in war plans—conventional or nuclear—lest the civilians tinker without possessing adequate expertise. That feeling has been especially strong with nuclear plans because they have been considered so essential to the nation's security.

Early in the nuclear era, this aversion to outside interference bordered on insubordination. General Curtis LeMay, commander of the Strategic Air Command from 1948 to 1957, felt so strongly that only he and his experts could formulate our nuclear strategic plans that for several years he failed to inform even the Joint Chiefs of Staff of changes he had made to those plans.[1] LeMay was an extremist, but his reluctance to share information on nuclear war plans persisted. Secretaries of defense, beginning with Robert McNamara in 1960, intruded more and more into this military province, but presidential involvement still was limited. For instance, until the early 1970s the Joint Chiefs of Staff did not brief any president on their annual nuclear war game, which estimated the outcome of a nuclear exchange with the Soviet Union, and then only did so largely because they believed the results would justify requests for more nuclear weapons.[2] In the late 1970s, President Carter made a diligent, personal effort to understand our nuclear position. By 1989, the balance had tipped sufficiently that President Bush, through Secretary of Defense Dick Cheney, put his hand directly on the targeting situation, eliminating thousands of unnecessary targets. And in 1991 he directly addressed numbers of weapons by unilaterally withdrawing almost all tactical nuclear weapons from deployed positions.

One reason this process took so long is that it has been neither necessary nor advantageous for a president to stir up the issue of reducing numbers of nuclear weapons. It was not necessary because all had confidence that they could control *any* release of nuclear weapons, no matter how many we had. Also, there was no political advantage to taking on the issue, only the risk of being painted as soft on communism and of challenging the proclivities of the military and military-industrial complex for more and more weapons. For example, President Carter's task of persuading the Senate to ratify SALT II would have been impossible had the Joint Chiefs of Staff opposed the treaty.

To get numbers under control despite the military's thirst for more weapons, all presidents since John Kennedy have turned more to arms control agreements with the Soviet Union and Russia rather than to internal reforms. At first these agreements constrained growth in the two arsenals, but later they led to reduced numbers and to actions to avoid accidental, unauthorized, and miscalculated use. The public has accepted the idea that continuing reductions through arms control agreements is the norm. For instance, unilateral moves by Presidents Bush and Clinton to reduce the risk of accidents were accepted as a matter of fact. What this means, I believe, is that additional presidential initiatives to curtail reliance on nuclear weapons could be well received. In the long run, progress in this direction could stand out as a president's mark for posterity—the enduring impact on humanity of reducing the risk of nuclear devastation.

To effect substantial change in nuclear policies, a president would have to reshape the bureaucracies. A president needs to be the driving force to overcome strong bureaucratic dedication to the traditional precepts of nuclear strategy. Most of those precepts, such as more is always better, have never been sound. The fact that they persisted throughout the entire Cold War gave them the false appearance of validity. A president, then, would do well to break down the current bureaucratic system, which still is heavily influenced by those precepts. To appreciate why this is a problem, we need to return to Clausewitz's dictum that war is a continuation of policy by other means, that is, that the nation's political aims govern decisions on preparing for and conducting war.

Clausewitz, however, was vague on just how to divide those decisions between political and military authorities: He said that "operational details [like] the posting of guards or the employment of patrols" should not be a matter for political decision.[3] That is adequate advice at the lower, tactical end of the spectrum of military decisionmaking. As we move toward the higher, strategic end, however, we need to elaborate on Clausewitz, because political factors become increasingly important. Thus, we need a new maxim: *Any military decision with significant implications for policy must be based on significant guidance from political authorities.* When it comes to nuclear weapons, almost every decision in peace or war fits that formula. For example: The numbers and types of nuclear weapons in our arsenal threaten others in a way no amount of conventional weaponry could; the doctrine enunciated for using them signals a frightening intent; and any use of even one nuclear weapon after a half-century tradition of nonuse would have untold implications for humankind.

This is not to say there has not been a shift away from the dominant role the military played in nuclear strategy under General LeMay. Our decision process does place control of all decisions on nuclear weapons in the hands of civilian policymakers, and they are exercising that authority more today than even ten years ago. Specific targets are proposed by the commander in chief of the Strategic Command in Omaha based on broad objectives set out by the secretary of defense. Recommended targets are then approved or disapproved by the secretary. The Strategic Command, however, is inclined to favor military targets and ways to gain favorable exchange ratios.

Although these are not necessarily bad practices for winning conventional wars, "winning" a nuclear war is quite a different matter. At the upper extreme, if we were pushed past our point of non-recovery, there could be no victor. Our objective in retaliating would be to push the opponent past its point of non-recovery also. That would not be a matter of exchange ratios or numbers of targets destroyed but of an imprecise amount of societal and economic disruption that cumulatively would bring society to a prolonged halt. At the lower end, say, a limited nuclear attack, the success of our retaliation would still not be measured in amounts of destruction but in whether the enemy understood from our controlled response that the consequences of continuing would be more disastrous than capitulation.

Between these two extremes—limited, demonstrative controlled response and the societal destruction of non-recovery—there are various levels of nuclear exchanges. Nowhere on that spectrum is the amount of physical destruction the appropriate criterion. Rather, since we would lose more with every exchange, our measure of success should be the earliest termination on favorable terms. How we use force to bring that about is not a military matter but a political judgment. All across the spectrum, then, from very controlled to very wide nuclear responses, the desired effects are measured in political terms more than in military terms—not in how much is destroyed but in how quickly the opponent understands that policy objectives cannot be fulfilled by continuing to wage nuclear war. It is neither wise nor fair to charge *military* planners with drawing up plans tailored more to *political* concerns. The last thing we should want is to encourage the military to set the political objectives of war.

How could we revamp our decision process to take better account of policy objectives? The locus for selecting targets, weapons, and delivery vehicles could be shifted even more toward policymakers in the Department of Defense. For instance, targets intended for controlled responses should be selected by those who best understand the culture, psychology, and personal factors influencing specific foreign leaders or leadership elites; targets intended to push an opponent past non-recovery should be selected on the basis of analyses of economic and societal effects by those with such expertise. In the past, given the thousands upon thousands of targets and the requirement for precisely timing the arrival of warheads, it took the immense computer capabilities at the Strategic Command to pull together 1 million pages of war plans. But if we are talking about only 250 targets (enough to cause the non-recovery of Russia and China, more than enough as to other countries of concern), the problem is more manageable.

The Strategic Command still needs to be intimately involved, but only in certifying delivery, probability, and accuracy. The end product would be a menu of options—selected by civilian policymakers and vetted by the Strategic Command—from which any president could choose according to the circumstances. In recent years, the Department of Defense has been moving in this direction by creating more options within set war plans. Despite these, our doctrine for using nuclear weapons to achieve favorable exchange ratios and our sense of urgency to respond before more of our own forces are attacked have made it likely that a president would be pressured into a set war plan with a large number of nuclear weapons. We need to escape the burden of preset plans altogether. Presidents should construct their own war plans from the menus of options they and their advisers have created in advance.

By asking policymakers to play an even larger role in selecting targets there is a danger of merely handing authority from one bureaucracy to another, one that might be equally disposed to the traditional precepts of nuclear strategy. After all, civilian experts on nuclear strategy developed many of these questionable precepts in the first place. To avoid this, the civilian authorities who develop targeting menus must reflect the policy views of the president. One way to ensure this is to create a second, presidentially appointed position of deputy secretary of defense, exclusively for nuclear security. This would effectively divide the Pentagon into nuclear and nonnuclear sides. Only the Joint Chiefs of Staff and various support elements would be on both sides. There would, of course, be areas of overlap, for example, attack submarines or strategic bombers with both conventional and nuclear missions. Overlap problems are manageable by establishing ground rules. For example, a commander of attack submarines with a conventional mission would not be allowed to remove nuclear weapons from them or send them out of their assigned theaters without permission from the deputy secretary of defense for nuclear security; a commander of strategic bombers would not be allowed to send them on a conventional mission without the agreement of the deputy secretary. It would also be useful to consolidate a single budget for all nuclear forces under this deputy secretary rather than put pieces in the budgets of the military services, as at present. The tradeoffs between nuclear and conventional forces should be at this higher level, because under a policy of no first-use they are not interchangeable; the preference of the services for conventional forces also often gets in the way of sound decisions.

Overall, such a realignment of responsibilities would drive home two points: that we would never introduce nuclear weapons into a conventional war, even as a last resort; and that in the event of being forced to use nuclear weapons in retaliation to a nuclear attack we would not automatically resort to traditional rules for fighting but would use controlled responses under the direction of policymakers. One hopes that having a presidential appointee with no responsibilities other than nuclear matters would not only ensure that the president's views were accurately reflected in policies and actions but also encourage greater presidential involvement in the entire decision process.

A president seeking to instill a new philosophy as to nuclear weapons would also do well to establish a system of checks from outside the Department of Defense. Bureaucratic organizations are not only resistant to change but also expert at stifling imaginative ideas and dissenting views. Moreover, decisions on nuclear forces, policies, and uses are so important that a president should hear several points of view, including those of people who have no bureaucratic axes to grind. One way to get such wide-ranging advice to a president is to create a Presidential Council for Nuclear Security composed of seven individuals from outside the government serving part-time expressly for this purpose, plus the Secretaries of Defense, State, and Energy; the head of the Arms Control and Disarmament Agency; the chairman of the Joint Chiefs of Staff; and the Director of Central Intelligence.

These thirteen—six insiders plus seven outsiders including the chair—would constitute the president's top advisory body on all decisions concerning nuclear weapons: procurement, targeting plans, peacetime deployment, and wartime operations. They would act sort of like a corporate board of directors, with a mix of insiders with detailed knowledge and outsiders with more detached objectivity. The council would have a modest staff to do fact-finding independent of the bureaucracies. It would enjoy access to all information on nuclear matters and would attempt to ensure that the president's policies were, in fact, being carried out. The body would meet periodically with the National Security Council to ensure nuclear policy was in harmony with other military and political policies. During a potential nuclear crisis, the Council for Nuclear Security and the National Security Council would meet jointly to advise the president.

These three steps—shifting targeting decisions to policymakers, creating the position of deputy secretary of defense for nuclear security, and establishing the Council for Nuclear Security—would accentuate the role that civilian advisers play over military advisers. That is not to say, however, that this would be a good idea for decisionmaking on conventional weapons. Giving greater responsibility to civilian policymakers in formulating nuclear strategy can be justified only by the fact that political factors dominate military factors, that is, decisions must be based more on political appraisal than on military technique. The disadvantage is that military advice is usually professional and consistent, whereas advice from a largely civilian council—especially one with a majority of non-government members—would likely fluctuate. Members would come and go, and the outsiders especially would need time to gain experience and expertise. The upside is that political policies deserve periodic reexamination, more so than military strategies, because there are fewer certainties (e.g., weapons performance data and standard tactics). A president, in selecting outside members, would want to strike a balance between those with established opinions and expertise in nuclear matters and those unfamiliar with the issues but with very inquiring minds. Most should share the president's basic philosophies on nuclear policies, but some should represent sufficiently differing views to give the council respectability in the eyes of the American public.

An additional step would be to return to the earlier practice of assigning custody of all nuclear warheads to the Department of Energy. In the majority of cases, this would be nominal, as the Department of Energy would have to suballocate warheads actually deployed in operational units to the Department of Defense. Energy, however, would be entitled to oversee the controls on those warheads, for example, the number in each silo, submarine, and storage bunker on strategic bomber bases. Energy would also assume physical custody of all warheads not deployed with an operational unit, including excess units awaiting dismantling, units in transit, and units being used for reliability inspections. This practice would help establish the principle that nuclear weapons are not military property to be employed in war-fighting.

The president would need support from Congress to implement these initiatives. Congressional involvement in nuclear issues began with the formation of the Joint Committee on Atomic Energy in 1942; it was very active initially but disbanded in 1977. Congressional jurisdiction over nuclear weapons was assumed by the House and Senate committees on armed services, which have created subcommittees on nuclear matters. Their roles have been more of supervisory observation than of positive direction. The issues are complex, there is minimal constituent interest in the topic, and there always loomed the risk of being painted as soft on communism. The end of the Cold War mitigates the last factor, but the other two remain problematic for members.

Another point to consider when discussing the role of Congress is the pressure members receive from the military-industrial lobby to build more expensive nuclear delivery systems, like bombers and submarines. With nuclear force levels clearly on the decline, there will be less of this pressure. Additionally, when steps to reduce the federal deficit bite into the defense budget, the military services will be more willing to reduce nuclear force levels than conventional ones. In any event, Congress traditionally has insisted that we keep pace with the Soviets in terms of numbers; whether this will continue in regard to the Russians is difficult to forecast. The composition of Congress is changing. More than half of the members in the Senate and two-thirds in the House have never served in the military; in the 1996 electoral campaign, defense issues did not figure prominently. We must have hope that a few leaders in each chamber will encourage adequate attention to the reshaping of U.S. nuclear policy.

To stimulate reform, Congress could establish separate committees on nuclear security, something not very different from having subcommittees. But creating full committees would accentuate the philosophy that nuclear weapons are more political instruments than military ones. There would be a clear risk, however, of seeing these committees become bastions of support for more nuclear weapons, as was the case with the Joint Committee on Atomic Energy. In my view, that is a risk we should take: The elected representatives of the people must be active and full participants in decisions as vital as those on nuclear matters.

In addition, Congress should appropriate all funds for procuring and maintaining nuclear weapons to a single department. Currently, appropriations for the Department of Energy cover laboratory research, development, testing, and production of nuclear weapons; those for the Department of Defense cover all operational aspects. Over the years, this division has had the insidious effect of encouraging the Department of Defense to be somewhat cavalier about asking for more and different kinds of nuclear weapons, as it has not had to pay for developing and producing them. The more practical solution would be to consolidate all these moneys in the defense budget. Defense would, then, reimburse the Department of Energy for services rendered. The opposite solution— putting everything in the energy budget—would have the merit of emphasizing the nonmilitary role of nuclear weapons, but it would likely be unacceptable to the Department of Defense.

Evolutionary changes in established bureaucratic processes simply become absorbed. Revolutionary change, because it is unsettling, can throw the bureaucrats off base just long enough to give the changes a chance to survive.

10

THE SINE QUA NON–
CITIZEN SUPPORT

In July 1995, in the course of doing research for this book, I visited the Strategic Command at Offutt Air Force Base outside Omaha, Nebraska. My key objective was to see how nuclear policy had changed since my last visit, in 1980 as Director of Central Intelligence. Back then, I was comparing the views at Offutt as to the balance of strategic forces with those at the CIA. They were pretty much in line, that is, the Soviets were improving their strategic nuclear forces and could well tip the balance in their favor, leaving us vulnerable to a preemptive attack; we needed to maintain parity so as to be able to "cover" all the targets that Soviet strategic forces presented.

An analysis, to which I subscribed, showing there was no possible window of vulnerability had not been accepted by the experts at CIA, and certainly not at Offutt. That analysis depended heavily on the assumption that U.S. SSBNs were quite invulnerable. I could see why that was an unpopular view at Offutt. The general on whom I called commanded the Strategic Air Command, an Air Force command with ICBMs and bombers. The other strategic nuclear force, Navy SSBNs, was controlled from Norfolk, Virginia, by an admiral. There was a rear admiral stationed at Offutt to ensure coordination of the two forces. It was this overall, co-ordinated posture that interested me, but my arranged schedule did not include a visit with the admiral and his staff. SAC was a proud, parochial command. I went away, however, wondering if the unique capabilities of

SSBNs were being adequately considered (e.g., how there possibly could be a window of vulnerability).

When I returned fifteen years later, I knew important changes had been made. In 1992, SAC was abolished in favor of the Strategic Command, which incorporated operational control of Navy SSBNs with Air Force ICBMs and bombers. Accordingly, StratCom is to be commanded alternately by an Air Force general and a Navy admiral. All this seemed to be considerable progress. The man who had been a moving force behind this change, Air Force General Lee Butler, had retired but was living in Omaha. While in town I called on him. As mentioned earlier, when he first arrived he found some 12,000-plus targets among the one million pages of war plans. He and his superiors in the Pentagon eliminated 75 percent of them—a prodigious accomplishment. He mentioned he had dropped many bridges from the target list, and I assumed the Bulgarian railroad bridge that first piqued my interest in nuclear targeting was among them.

I knew also of the growing ferment outside Omaha among prominent civilians and retired generals and admirals: former Secretary of Defense Robert S. McNamara; former Deputy Secretary of Defense Paul H. Nitze; General Butler; former Supreme Allied Commander in Europe General Andrew J. Goodpaster; and former commander of the U.S. Space Command General Charles Horner. These and more were sounding the alarm over the excessive numbers of nuclear weapons—not only in our arsenal but in others as well.*

The fact that Butler, Goodpaster, and Horner were involved in this was particularly significant to me. They had been direct participants in nuclear policy and yet had come to this conclusion. Surprisingly, at least to those outside the military, very few senior military officers have such a grasp of nuclear strategy or any interest in it. (Remember that I was already a rear admiral when I first learned how shockingly many warheads were in the SIOP.) A small club of zealous military experts has dominated the military's input on nuclear weapons policy. The members of this club have insisted on parity with Russia, on being ready to fight it out even with large numbers of weapons, and on agonizing over a window of vul-

---

*In December 1996, some sixty retired admirals and generals from fourteen countries (including nineteen from the United States, eighteen from Russia, four from the United Kingdom, and one from France) banded together and signed a manifesto recommending nuclear disarmament.

nerability. As recently as 1994, they successfully twisted the Nuclear Posture Review into a meaningless effort.

As I went into the briefing room at StratCom on my return visit, I wondered where these people stood between the new thinking of Generals Butler, Goodpaster, and Horner and the old thinking of General LeMay. It was quickly obvious: Comparative numbers still mattered very much, although the fixation was weaker than it had been in 1980. The START II level of 3,500 warheads was a bare minimum to "cover" what we needed to cover; we could tolerate going down to 3,500 only if we held a reserve that allowed us to build back up. Despite the malaise within Russia, they suspected the Russians were surreptitiously diverting resources to new nuclear capabilities. In answering my specific question, they did not think 3,500 warheads could bring Russia to its knees, that is, to its point of non-recovery, because it is so large. Their calculations took into account only the individual targets destroyed, for example, a factory, a military headquarters, or an ICBM silo—and did not account for the impact on the other elements of the society and economy of losing these services. They had never heard of the MIT study that showed that 250 warheads targeted on U.S. liquid fuel supplies could carry our country to non-recovery.

The job at Offutt was to meet the broad criteria for targeting set down by the secretary of defense, for example, to destroy some percentage of all industry or of all ICBMs with high assurance. What the total effect on Russia would be was beyond their concern. As the meeting went on I asked, provocatively, "What if we would only target key points in the Russian industrial system, even if they were in cities—could we not do with a lot fewer weapons?" An officer was instantly dispatched with instructions to bring the command's legal officer to join us. He explained that targeting innocent civilians in cities was against international law. The generals in the room chimed in for good measure that the American public would not stand for such a targeting plan. The legal officer then was straightforward in completing the picture: If our cities were attacked first, the law sanctioned retaliation in kind. The nuance, apparently, was that in peacetime it was illegal to draw up plans to target civilians, which left military targets or the sophistry that something like a power plant in the middle of a city did not involve innocent civilians. But if the Russians attacked first and hit our cities—as would be almost inevitable—well, then, all bets were off. Since I could not imagine the United States starting a nuclear war with Russia, it looked like the legal point was an academic excuse to help justify larger forces. It also fit General LeMay's thesis that we might go first.

I left feeling that despite all the changes that had taken place since Curtis LeMay left SAC in 1957, his influence on StratCom was much stronger than was Lee Butler's.

SECRECY IN A DEMOCRATIC GOVERNMENT is an anathema. This applies to the necessary secrecy of intelligence operations, to military war plans and equipment, to illegal or improper activities of the government itself—and to nuclear strategy. Nowhere in our government has secrecy been more profound than with respect to nuclear weapons. The great emphasis on secrecy concerning the Manhattan Project back in 1942 was easy to understand. After all, we saw ourselves in a race with Germany on which the fate of the free world would hinge. This carried over into the Cold War. Information about nuclear weapons was one of the first to be secluded in a special compartment above "Top Secret" labeled "Restricted Data." Access could be had only with a special permit.

A partial result of this compartmentation of information is that presidents and the Congress have played a less active role in formulating nuclear strategy compared to most any other policy of comparable import and expense. Even within the military, access to information on nuclear weapons has been severely restricted. Under these circumstances, it is no wonder citizens have not been well-informed. Indeed, they have been misinformed. Many civilian and military experts who shaped policy on nuclear weapons simply lost focus. They became myopic in the wealth of technical detail and in the intellectual challenge of reconciling irreconcilables, or they gave way to parochial interests of the military services or military industry.

This is not to say that these experts did not also do a service to the country in bringing us through the Cold War without a nuclear detonation, but an additional result is a legacy of sophistic theories to which much of the media and the public subscribe. These never made sense even when first formulated, for example, windows of vulnerability; the importance of parity; the necessity of a TRIAD of nuclear forces; and plans to escalate nuclear war until we dominated—no matter what the damage to our country. If ever scrutiny by the public was needed because scrutiny by the bureaucracy was so limited, this was it.

In my opinion, the public would never have accepted 32,500 nuclear warheads as a sensible proposition. Others argue that public reaction could have been just the opposite, that is, to endorse and reinforce the experts. It is not important which thesis is correct, because citizen input wherever possible is an essential ingredient of our form of government. Today, that input should be greater. Much of what was Restricted Data is out in the open, and much more could be. There are only two sectors where secrecy on nuclear weapons remains necessary. One is on how we sustain the invulnerability of our retaliatory forces. Until we move away from deterrence by threat of retaliation, our confidence in the invulnerability of those forces is the key to not panicking during a crisis. The other is on advanced techniques for making nuclear weapons. The basic equations are readily available, but we do not want other data that would simplify the task to reach the hands of would-be proliferators. Iraq, for instance, was forced to follow some cumbersome processes for refining fissionable material in searching for nuclear capability.

Within these limits, we need to devise ways to involve our citizens more. This means overcoming the public apathy on this subject since the end of the Cold War. One approach would be for the government to publish more information to help the public grasp essential elements in the nuclear field. For example:

- A guide to the lethality of nuclear weapons could be produced in the language of nonexperts. This would have to grapple with the historical problem of government underestimation, at the least describing areas of uncertainty and differing theories about the resulting effects.
- Data could be released on the problems others face in manufacturing nuclear weapons, and the state of progress of various aspirant countries. There would be objections that releasing data on other countries would compromise our intelligence sources. This need not be the case, however. If the data we published were in error by some modest amount because we either withheld or lacked some sensitive information, it would be assumed we were merely not telling all.

- Information could be assembled on the past, present, and future costs of U.S. programs for nuclear weapons. This would enable the public to place nuclear programs in perspective with other national needs. This should include the costs of repairing damage to the environment.
- Perhaps most important of all, statistics could be released on the risks we have taken and are taking. The government should publish a summary of key U.S. war plans for the Cold War era, estimating the deaths and damage they would have brought to others. The public needs to understand the extremes to which we went and that we want to avoid in the future. It should also summarize the impact of what we believe the Soviet Union's key war plans against the United States would have been, or, if the Russians would cooperate, their own estimates of such impact. Citizens need to understand the risks of nuclear war.

Much of this information is already available from official government sources or from materials pieced together by private organizations. What is needed is the authenticity of a governmental presentation and, hopefully, a clarity of statement that is so often missing in this field. One of the problems is that no government organization feels a responsibility for informing the public on nuclear matters. A department or agency should be assigned the responsibility, after coordinating with the other agencies involved, of providing the public as much information as possible. The culture of secrecy in the Department of Defense is too strong for it to be tasked with this. The Department of State lacks the necessary expertise. But the Department of Energy and the Arms Control and Disarmament Agency are qualified, and either could do the job well.

Publishing data, of course, would merely lay the foundation for stimulating public debate. There are those who argue doing so would elevate the importance of nuclear weapons, frightening rather than reassuring citizens. Letting the government decide what citizens should know, other than on grounds of secrecy, would be a greater risk. Once the basic data are available, the government's resources for engaging the public in debate on it are awesome. They start, of course, with the president's involvement and commitment—speeches, remarks to the press, and requests to the Congress ranging from resolutions of national intent to new laws to the ratification of treaties.

Once a president is engaged, many other resources will flow: speeches by other officials, conferences, videos, publications, and encouragement to private organizations, perhaps by organizing speaking engagements.

The private sector also has almost endless opportunities for galvanizing public interest. The media naturally will key off speeches and press conferences. The more responsible leadership in the media will recognize the importance of a topic like this and encourage attention to it. Private foundations, and the activities they support through institutes, councils, study groups, and individual writing efforts, are also very important. There is a particular problem today in that many foundations and institutes have shifted their focus from national security to domestic issues. This is understandable and in many ways justified. The issues of peace and war still plague us, however, and the specter of nuclear war will be a constant concern. We need a few private foundations and organizations that recognize the vital importance of U.S. nuclear weapons policies.

But government leadership *and* private efforts will be needed to overcome the public's post–Cold War apathy. There is also the American public's record of not wanting to fall behind the Russians. We need a more sophisticated understanding of what inferiority and superiority mean in this unique arena. That will be well worth engendering, because it would become part of a more sophisticated public understanding that in the post–Cold War world the United States can afford to take bold steps such as those being proposed in my new vision for nuclear stability. Our position of prominence at this time permits it.

We would, of course, be foolish to assume our prominent position will continue forever. Instead, we should look for opportunities to move the United States, Russia, and the world community in constructive directions—but without imposing our will in ways that sow seeds of resentment. Moving toward this new vision of nuclear stability would be one of the most constructive moves we could make. Convincing the American public we can do it would be a big step toward a post–Cold War maturity in American thinking. The initial momentum for going in such a direction must come from the president. Presidents, however, will not be the point person for long unless there is strong public interest.

The most important dividend of the Cold War is still there to be reaped. Ultimately, it will be us—the citizens—who determine whether we reap it.

APPENDIX A:
LETHALITY OF NUCLEAR WEAPONS

The executive branch of our government has been negligent, even irresponsible, in underestimating the impact nuclear weapons would have. A good example of this is data derived by the Department of Defense and presented to Congress in March 1974 by Secretary of Defense James R. Schlesinger. In discussing the fatalities we might sustain in a Soviet attack against our nuclear forces, Schlesinger stated, "I am talking here about casualties of 15,000, 20,000, 25,000."[1] Six months later, Schlesinger revised that figure to the order of 1.5 million.[2] In another ten months, the Department of Defense, in a written response to Congress, revised the estimate upward to 3.2 million to 16.3 million. A survey conducted by the Congress's Office of Technology Assessment (OTA) found that an attack similar in dimension would most likely result in the deaths of 14 million people. Independent analysis using more sophisticated damage estimation models has resulted in significantly greater casualty estimates. One done by Princeton University's Center for Energy and Environmental Studies concluded that 7 million to 25 million people would die. This variation in estimated fatalities from 15,000 to 25 million is typical of the indifferent way in which the government has approached this subject.

Indifference is abetted by the shorthand terminology employed when dealing with the quantities of power involved in nuclear weaponry. It is simply difficult to write about a "one billion, one hundred million pound bomb," or to use endless zeros (e.g., "a 1,100,000,000 pound bomb"). Yet those are the only ways to describe a nuclear weapon that permit a fair comparison with the norm we hold—conventional bombs that range from 500 to 2,000 pounds. For convenience, we talk in terms of megatons (MT, millions of tons) or kilotons (KT, thousands of tons).

If START II is implemented, the standard intercontinental warhead in the Russian inventory will be 550 KT, that is, 550 × 1,000 (kilo) × 2,200 (lbs./metric tonne), or 1,210,000,000 pounds. It would take more than 25,000 sorties by our most modern bomber, the B-2, to deliver that much explosive in conventional munitions. It would take a freight train 150 miles long to transport it to the airfield.[3] Another comparison is that in the course of some 44,000 aircraft sorties during the six-week air campaign in the Gulf War with Iraq in 1991, we dropped about 84,000 tonnes of conventional bombs,[4] or less than one-fifth of the explosive equivalent of a single 550-KT nuclear bomb.

But there is a particular danger in this terminology: It becomes not so incongruous to talk about "small" nuclear warheads. When we label them as being "only" .1 KT, a warhead that would fit on an artillery shell, it sounds small. But .1 KT is the equivalent of .1 × 1,000 (kilo) × 2,200 (lbs./tonne), or 220,000 pounds of conventional explosive. One of the smallest warheads we have had in our inventory was a .1-KT artillery shell, but the power of one such shell was the equivalent, in conventional explosives, of five fully loaded B-2 bombers. Another perspective: "Three 1-MT nuclear explosions would release the same amount of energy as all bombs dropped in the six years of World War II."[5]

The danger of terminology leading to our misunderstanding lethality is compounded by the fact that these comparisons of tonnages consider only blast effects, which are all there is when talking about conventional munitions. But blast effects are only the beginning when talking about nuclear weapons. The additional effects of nuclear weapons are: thermal energy, radioactivity, electromagnetic pulse, economic and societal disruption, and environmental damage. These can greatly increase the total effect.

It is in the area of these effects unique to nuclear weapons that the Executive Branch has not been sufficiently persevering. There are different reasons for each instance of underestimating or ignoring these effects.

Blast Effect

The detonation of a nuclear weapon creates a ball of superheated air that initially expands outward at millions of miles per hour. This expanding "fireball" acts like a fast-moving piston on the surrounding air, creating a shell of compressed air—the "shockwave"—of enormous power and extent. The shockwave propagates outward by pressing against the next layer of air, crushing that layer into a shell of air that in turn presses against the air layer beyond. This process leads not only to the forward motion of the shell of high-pressure air but also to high winds due to the inevitable flow of air from each successive layer to the next.

The shockwave can be thought of as having an "overpressure" or "static overpressure" that can crush objects in its path, and a "dynamic overpressure" due to the accompanying high winds, that can knock down and tear apart structures. In general, large, well-constructed buildings are destroyed by the hammerlike effect of the arriving shockwave and the crushing effect of overpressure as the shock envelops the structure. In contrast, objects like trees and utility poles are not always susceptible to damage from the crushing effects of the pressure wave but are, instead, destroyed by the high winds that accompany the shock.[6]

As a shockwave passes over a target area it carries heavy objects lifted by the accompanying winds, and it will cause the damage or collapse of structures from the combined effects of high winds, the smashing effects of objects being carried by the winds, and the hammering and crushing effects of overpressure. Individuals may be killed, injured, or trapped as the structures around them collapse; if they are caught in the open they might be hit by wind-carried objects or be picked up and carried by the wind and thrown up against walls and the like. The pressure wave can thereby cause many deaths and injuries by numerous mechanisms that will depend on the luck or luckless circumstance of each victim in its path.

As an illustration, a shockwave from a nuclear explosion that generates five pounds per square inch (psi) static overpressure will be accompanied by winds of 160 miles per hour (mph). At Hiroshima and Nagasaki, the 5 psi range was a "lethal zone" for humans within which 50 percent were killed and some 30 percent more injured. At the 5 psi range, unreinforced brick and lesser buildings were destroyed; 200 to 600 bits per square yard of debris and shards of glass were sent flying about with lethal effect. A modern 550-KT nuclear bomb would generate such winds and a static overpressure of 5 psi out to 3.5 miles if the burst were in the air (that is, if the detonation were high enough that the fireball did not touch the ground).

If burst in contact with the ground, a 550-KT weapon would generate 5 psi out to only 2.3 miles; to a range of about 1.1 miles from ground zero the overpressure would be 20 psi and the winds more than 500 mph—sufficient to destroy many reinforced concrete structures. A groundburst weapon will maximize damage at ground zero and create extensive radiation effects, whereas an airburst will maximize the area affected by blast damage.

The executive branch employs a straightforward "cookie cutter" model to calculate overpressures for various nuclear detonations at various ranges from ground zero. It then scales the known casualty rates for those overpressures at Hiroshima to the population and nature of the area under consideration.

One way to place these data in perspective is to recognize that in terms of blast today's 550-KT weapon has forty times the yield of the one employed at Hiroshima.˙ Although scaling up by this much has its risks, the executive branch's estimates of blast effect seem reasonable.

Executive branch estimates do, however, ignore one effect of blast: "blast disruption fires." These fires may be started by ruptured natural gas lines, overturned electrical equipment with resulting short circuits, and other disrupted flammable facilities such as stoves, furnaces, and gasoline pumps. Here, the extent of fires would be dependent on the particular locale. Although blast disruption fires potentially could substantially enhance the damage from a nuclear explosion, many more fires will on average be set by the intense light flash from the fireball, discussed next.

Thermal Energy

The fireball created by a nuclear explosion will be much hotter than the surface of the sun for fractions of a second and will radiate light and heat, as do all objects of very high temperature. Because the fireball is so hot and close to the earth, it will deliver enormous amounts of heat and light to the terrain surrounding the detonation point, and it will be hundreds or thousands of times brighter than the sun at noon. If the fireball is created by the detonation of a 1-MT nuclear weapon, for example, within roughly eight- to nine-tenths of a second each section of its surface will be radiating about three times as much heat and light as a comparable area of the sun itself. The intense flash of light and heat from the explosion of a 550-KT weapon can carbonize exposed skin and cause clothing to ignite. At a range of three miles, for instance, surfaces would fulminate and recoil as they emanate flames, and even particles of sand would explode like pieces of popcorn from the rapid heating of the fireball. At three and a half miles, where the blast pressure would be about 5 psi, the fireball could ignite clothing on people, curtains and upholstery in homes and offices, and rubber tires on cars. At four miles, it could blister aluminum surfaces, and

---

*A yield 40 times greater does not result in 40 times as much destruction. A 1-MT weapon has 1,000 times the destructive yield of a 1-KT weapon, but the blast effects cover only 100 times as much area, although the thermal and radiation effects would be approximately 600–900 times as great.

at six to seven miles it could still set fire to dry leaves and grass. This flash of incredibly intense, nuclear-driven sunlight could simultaneously set an uncountable number of fires over an area of close to 100 square miles.

In executive branch estimates the range of lethal thermal effect is calculated by using the same scaling factor as with blast effect. This method, however, disregards the fact that the range of thermal effects scales up faster with increased weapon yield than do blast effects. Thus, weapons larger than that employed at Hiroshima will set fires and burn people at greater distances than the blast effect will kill them.

The lethality of thermal effects depends on weather (clear or murky), but uncertainties due to weather variations, surprisingly, are not larger than the uncertainties in blast effects. Simply speaking, the variations in blast effects tend to be deemphasized and ignored, yet the government argues that variations in thermal effects make them difficult to predict.

Another serious thermal effect on urban areas is the firestorm that will follow. This firestorm results from the many fires initiated by the intense light and heat thrown off by the fireball. Executive branch estimates of casualties from nuclear attacks ignore this lethal consequence of nuclear attack: "Due to the large area of the fire, the fire zone would act as a gigantic air pump, driving enormous volumes of air skyward. As cooler air is drawn in to replace the air pumped away, the pumping action would create very high ground winds. Large amounts of poisonous smoke and gases would be generated and could therefore kill many more people than blast effects alone."[7] During World War II, firestorms resulting from incendiary bombings devastated Tokyo and Dresden; firestorms consumed Hiroshima and Nagasaki as a result of nuclear attacks.

"Conflagration" models developed to estimate damage and deaths from all kinds of fires conclude there will be 1.5–4.1 times more deaths than the executive branch estimates. These results have been rejected on the grounds that in any particular circumstance they are dependent on the amount of moisture in combustible materials in the area, the local weather and atmospheric visibility, and other factors that will influence the likelihood of fire ignitions (snow cover during winter or large amounts of dry underbrush during summer). These may well be cause to accept the low end of the 1.5–4.1 prediction as minimal for planning purposes—but not to ignore the consideration. One specific study that postulated 100 1-MT attacks on U.S. cities estimated that using blast effects only, there would be about 14 million fatalities; employing conflagration models would increase that to 23–56 million, depending on the assumptions.[8]

Finally, executive branch estimates of thermal casualties are low because many of the survivors with burns would die for lack of medical treatment. There are, for instance, specialized facilities for treating only about 2,000 burn victims in the entire country.[9] Moreover, people with burns might also have received high doses of radiation. Radiation exposure would depress their immune systems and greatly increase the probability of death from the complications of both burns and damage to immune systems.

Radioactivity

When matter is converted into energy, by either fission or fusion, one result is gamma radiation that is delivered in the form of electromagnetic waves similar to light and X-rays but with greater ability to penetrate materials. Another type of harmful radiation that is generated by nuclear explosives is neutron radiation, which is delivered as a "particle of unit mass."* These radioactive emissions have both prompt and delayed effects on people and the environment.

Prompt radiation from either an airburst or groundburst consists of gamma rays and neutrons emitted within the first minute. In high concentrations they can endanger humans. The general rule is that this radioactivity would be immediately fatal to humans only out to about where the individuals would die anyway from blast or thermal effects, although this is not true for weapons below 20 KT.[10] Executive branch estimates of deaths do take prompt radiation into account.

Delayed radiation, often called "fallout," occurs when a nuclear explosion takes place on the ground or at low altitude. Since the explosion derives its energy from nuclear reactions, large amounts of radioactive materials are created as a by-product of these reactions. When a detonation occurs at or near the ground, these radioactive materials get sucked into the rising fireball and become mixed with other debris. The rising fireball eventually carries these radioactive materials into the upper atmosphere, from where they are then deposited back minutes, hours, or days after the explosion. The groundburst of a 550-KT weapon can create a contaminated crater 800 feet in diameter and 165 feet deep. In so doing, hundreds of thousands of tons of dirt are lifted along with the radioactive materials from the bomb and thrust together upward. The heavier pieces of dirt carrying radioactive materials will fall back to earth within hours or days, creating a radiation hazard at significant distances from ground zero. For instance, a 500-KT groundburst could deliver enough radiation sixty to seventy miles downwind to kill all unprotected people within days if they did not take shelter or evacuate the area. Thirty miles downwind the outcome could be the same within four to five hours of the explosion.

A related example is the nonnuclear explosion, fire, and radioactive release in the nuclear power plant at Chernobyl in 1986. As a result of this accident, 1,200 square miles adjacent to the reactor were so contaminated that humans are still excluded; some 30,000 square miles of farmland can be only partially cultivated. The lighter radioactive particles can be carried on the winds as they decay or eventually be deposited back on earth as radioactive fallout over weeks or months and at distances of thousands of miles. For example, Chernobyl delivered mild contamination from fallout as far as northern Norway, some 1,500 miles distant.

There are many structures in Russia and the United States that have some level of blast resistance. In order to account for the higher blast resistance of these structures, we can detonate nuclear weapons at lower altitudes. For example, if an airfield contained aircraft shelters that were able to resist a 100-psi blast (aircraft shelters are usually considerably harder than this) a 550-KT weapon would have to be detonated at an altitude of less than a half-mile in order to maximize damage. Under these conditions, even though the detonation is not a surface burst, considerable fallout could be expected. This illustrates why it is likely that in a nuclear war with thousands of nuclear detonations, in all likelihood most such detonations would cause heavy fallout.

---

*L. W. McNaught, *Nuclear Weapons and Their Effects* (London: Brassey's Defence Publishers, 1984), p. 50. Two other forms of radiation are present during a nuclear explosion. These are alpha radiation, which can be stopped by a single sheet of paper, and beta radiation, which also has little penetrating power. These two forms of radiation are generally considered insignificant to the overall calculation of lethal effects in the event of a nuclear explosion.

There are models to estimate both the effects of fallout on people, and the size of any area near ground zero that will be contaminated. These models are built around the time of year, the prevailing weather patterns, and the type of protective measures individuals will take. In utilizing such models, the executive branch tends to assume an unrealistic degree of protection for the individual, for example, warning time to seek shelter; civil defense shelters, basements, or brick residences; whether people are willing to remain sheltered for weeks or even months; and whether supplies of food, water, and hygienic facilities have been prestocked. Perhaps the strongest reason to question whether the populace can be as protected as the government estimates is that the average citizen does not know how to seek protection. Civil defense has never caught on in our country. Thus, the thesis that survival would be greatly enhanced if people could keep several feet of dirt between them and any residual radioactivity for several weeks is less than useful.[11] The odds of getting massive numbers of Americans to understand civil defense and to practice it are nil.

The standard used in government estimates for human tolerance to radiation may also be overly optimistic, according to research on animals as well as data on residents of the Marshall Islands, who were accidentally irradiated in the test of a nuclear weapon.[12]

Further, government estimates are low because they are limited to fatalities that occur within the first thirty days following an attack. There clearly will be more deaths after that, and even during those first thirty days people with radiation sickness will be a drain on the process of recovery.

Another facet of radiation is the amount of land that would be contaminated by ground-bursts or low-altitude bursts, to the point it could not be inhabited for a considerable period of time. This could be in and around the crater at ground zero; it could also result from the immediate fallout in the nearby area or from later, more distant fallout. A 1-MT groundburst would, for instance, "result in the removal from cultivation of the equivalent of one million acres for seven years if the contaminated land were cultivated before the nuclear event."[13] The effect of being denied access to such sizable areas is not considered at all in executive branch estimates, largely because the amount and location of fallout are subject to many variables such as wind and weather. There is also no consideration of the fact that current and future food supplies would be at risk if the contaminated areas happened to be farmland. That, in turn, could raise psychological problems as people worried whether the food they were receiving was safe to eat.

Electromagnetic Pulse

EMP is an intense electric and magnetic pulse that is created by the gamma radiation that emanates from a nuclear detonation. The large electric fields created in this way produce high-voltage and current pulses in the electric circuits they encounter. These electric fields build to peak voltages many times faster than a lightning bolt, thereby overwhelming most devices that have been designed to protect electrical and electronic devices from surges in current and voltage. EMP from even a groundburst could knock out power grids, electrical equipment, and telephones as well as destroy computer memories six to twelve miles from ground zero (although not all such equipment would necessarily be damaged as the coupling of EMP is very dependent on many details of the circuits and not readily predictable). A burst at an altitude of 200 miles over Nebraska designed to produce EMP could shut down the national power grid, destroy computer memories, and knock out unprotected communications systems across the country.[14] EMP would affect the immediate ability of governmental authorities to manage the society, and repairing the damage would consume a considerable effort in the early reconstruction period. It is another area of neglect in executive branch estimates.

Environmental Effect

Since trees and many other plants are roughly as susceptible to radiation exposure as are people, any area exposed to levels of radiation high enough to kill or injure people would be deforested or depleted of plant life. This, in turn, would have implications for soil erosion and for the survival prospects of wild and domesticated animals (assuming that direct radiation exposure did not kill them outright). The sudden killing or stressing of some species by radiation could have unforeseen effects on the environmental balance. For example, insects, which are more resistant to radiation than birds, would no longer be subject to predation. This, in turn, could lead to wild fluctuations in the size of insect populations in the new ecological system created by the elimination of important predators and plant life.

Multiple nuclear explosions could also create sufficient nitric oxides to deplete the ozone layer twenty to thirty kilometers above the earth. This would expose humans and animals to higher-than-normal ultraviolet radiation. Although the physics of ozone depletion is not fully understood and cannot be quantified, the consequences of ozone depletion could be serious. There is also the thesis of "nuclear winter," in which vast fires started by an extensive nuclear attack would send sufficient smoke and particles into the atmosphere to cut off the sun for an extended period, with a subsequent cooling effect. Although the surface temperature might not change as severely as suggested by early predictions of nuclear winter, there are enough effects associated with this phenomenon that nuclear winter cannot be discounted entirely.

Economic and Social Disruption

The most serious area of underestimation by the executive branch is the disruptive effects on the economy and the society. It is the area that is most difficult to quantify. The effects of blast, thermal energy, fires, and radiation are measured by the number of fatalities and injured; the number of hardened structures, such as reinforced buildings or missile silos, destroyed; and the size of the area of soft structures leveled. Disruption of the economy and the society is measured by the interruption of services and supplies. These impact on far more than the area that has been attacked. Some examples with respect to the economy:

- If Chicago's railroad marshaling yards were destroyed, commerce moving across the country would be severely affected. Just how much would be determined by whether alternate routes, such as through St. Louis, have also been attacked.
- Much the same would be the case with one or several attacks on major airports. Our economy is highly dependent on rapid transportation, and there is little excess airport capacity.
- The disruption of Wall Street would bring the country's financial apparatus to a halt. Records of credit card and banking transactions and ownership of securities and properties could be destroyed.

- Attacks on our ICBM silos in the farm belt would contaminate farmland and crops. This, combined with disruptions in the food distribution network, could result in areas of starvation. Loss of agricultural productivity would also imperil our principal source of foreign exchange.
- Attacks on only a few harbors, refineries, and pipelines could deny the supply of crude oil into and throughout the country, resulting in crippling shortages of fuel for heating, automobiles, trucks, railroads, and industry.
- The interruption of supply chains due to fuel shortages, transportation bottlenecks, and the destruction of factories would ripple throughout our economy, which is finely tuned to "just in time" deliveries.
- The interruption of message communication links, computer networks, and electrical power grids by EMP would play havoc with economic activity across the board and with the government's effort of recovery.

There would also be equally serious problems in maintaining social cohesion:

- Federal, state, and local governments could have difficulty establishing sufficient communications to maintain order and direct the recovery effort.
- The contamination from even one bomb could displace hundreds of thousands of people and possibly lead to panic in evacuations—even looting and a general breakdown of law and order.
- With the death of perhaps half a million people over a period of just a few weeks in a single city from a single 1-MT nuclear blast, the loss of loved ones and the task of their burial would be psychologically traumatic. Moreover, it would seem never ending as radiation sickness gradually took its toll.
- Contamination of food supplies in rumor or fact could test civility and order.
- Fires could range on a scale that few fire departments could handle under normal conditions. In many cases, fire departments themselves would be destroyed, being without access to water supplies or simply unable to move through the rubble to where they are needed.
- Medical services could be stretched to the point that severe triage would be necessary. By government estimate, even if only one city were attacked by a single nuclear weapon, the remaining medical resources for the rest of the entire country would be inadequate to care for the half-million or so injured in that city, over and above those killed. And interruptions in water, electrical, and sanitation services could make the medical problem even worse and raise the specter of epidemics.

At some point, the overall psychological impact could be so great that society might not have the will to pull itself back together or, even if it did, the capability to do so. If the attacks are on only one or two cities, that is not likely to be the case. The Japanese reconstructed Hiroshima and Nagasaki reasonably quickly, and these have become relatively normal cities once again. The issue of ultimate recovery arises if there are more than only a few nuclear attacks, because damage to the society as a whole from two detonations would not be the sum of the two individual damages—but something greater. For instance, recovery at Hiroshima and Nagasaki was highly dependent on outside resources coming to the rescue. If many of the cities that helped Hiroshima and Nagasaki had also been attacked they too would have been seeking aid, not supplying it. At some number of detonations, sufficient sources of outside support would no longer be available to some areas. Each additional detonation would cut off more sources, until enough areas were hopelessly adrift that the society would fracture into regional societies and cease to function as a political and economic entity.

Overall Effect

There is no mathematical way to add up the effects of underestimation in all of the various areas mentioned above, and the total distortion would vary with the specific circumstances. My subjective evaluation, however, is that our government underestimates by a factor between two and eight.

TABLE A.1   Effects of Conventional and Nuclear Weapons

Effect	Conventional	Nuclear
Blast	✓	✓
Thermal Energy		✓
Radioactivity		✓
Electromagnetic Pulse		✓
Economic and Social Disruption		✓
Environmental Damage		✓

TABLE A.2   Summary of Executive Branch Estimating of the Effects of Nuclear Detonations

Effect	Estimated Satisfactorily	Under-estimated	Ignored
Blast			
Damage to property and people	✓		
Fires ignited by blast effects			✓
Thermal			
Direct ignition and burns fatal to people		✓	
Firestorms			✓
Radioactivity			
Prompt fatalities	✓		
Delayed fatalities from fallout			
Within 30 days		✓	
After 30 days			✓
Irradiation of ground areas			✓
Electromagnetic Pulse			
Disruption of electricity and communications			✓
Economic and Social Disruption			✓
Environmental Damage			
Depletion of plant life			✓
Ozone depletion			✓
Nuclear winter			✓

TABLE A.3   Blast Effects of a 550-KT Explosion 5,000 Feet Above the Earth

Distance from Ground Zero (miles)	Peak Overpressure (above atmosphere)	Peak Wind (mph)	Typical Effects
1.4	20 psi	507	Reinforced concrete structures leveled
2.2	10 psi	296	Most factories and commercial buildings collapse
3.3	5 psi	164	Lightly constructed commercial buildings destroyed; heavier construction severely damaged; houses collapse
4.5	3 psi	102	Walls of steel-frame buildings blown away; severe damage to residences; winds kill people in the open
8.7	1 psi	36	Damage to structures; people endangered by flying glass and debris

SOURCE: Adapted from U.S. Congress, Office of Technology Assessment, *The Effects of Nuclear War* (Washington, D.C.: Government Printing Office, 1990), p. 18.

APPENDIX B:
EXCERPTS FROM "NUCLEAR CRASH—
THE U.S. ECONOMY AFTER
SMALL NUCLEAR ATTACKS"

M. Anjali Sastry, Joseph J. Romm, Kosta Tsipis

The effects of a nuclear attack on a country's society and economy have been the subject of numerous studies based on data from the nuclear bombs used against Hiroshima and Nagasaki, from nuclear tests, and from conventional-bomb damage data.[1] Even though these studies have focused on quantitative calculations of the physical damage and have presented only qualitative extrapolations of the effects of this damage on the fate of the survivors, they were instrumental in establishing the fact that a nuclear exchange between two warring nations would result in tremendous devastation.

Studies done under government contract in the U.S. have until very recently shown that the U.S. economy can survive a limited nuclear attack. For example, a 1973 report by SRI on an input-output computer model simulation of the economy predicted complete economic recovery from a nuclear attack within a decade and a half—*regardless* of the attack size, which varied from 4% to 20% of the Soviet arsenal.

But very different results are reached by a 1980 systems dynamics computer model simulation of the post-attack U.S. economy that was commissioned by the Federal Emergency Management Agency (FEMA). The new FEMA model predicts the collapse of the U.S. economy following an attack much smaller than those SRI studied. To rebuild the economy to anything near its previous levels would take many decades.

If different models lead to different conclusions, how can one decide which one is best approximating the grim post-attack reality. We will examine both the SRI and FEMA models and show how the former was *bound* to give misleading results, while the latter was specifically designed to minimize or avoid many problems inherent in previous computer models of the post-attack economy.

Previous models were designed to operate within historical bounds, with the economy in equilibrium and so were unrealistic in their representation of the post-attack economy, which could very well be out of equilibrium for extended periods of time. Previous models have tended to be simple, linear, growth models that reproduce the historical behavior of the U.S. economy—sustained growth—almost immediately after much larger attacks than we consider here. The FEMA model, on the other hand, is designed to handle both equilibrium and non-equilibrium conditions. It is composed of hundreds of non-linear, recursive equations. And, while these equations reflect the historical performance of the economy, they are also designed to reflect specific actions taken by economic decision-makers (consumers, government officials, and corporate executives). Therefore, while the FEMA model can reproduce historical patterns, it is not "forced" to.

The technique the FEMA models uses, Systems Dynamics, is more interactive, more dynamic, and more flexible than methods previously used for simulations of the post-attack economy. In addition, we have based our analyses on: 1) the latest, most realistic estimates of the effects of nuclear weapons, 2) a detailed study of the distribution of key U.S. industries, and 3) an extensive Census Bureau database of U.S. population and manufacturing capacity. Nevertheless, the FEMA model is only a computer model, and while it may be more rigorous than the "mental" models we all use to anticipate the behavior of the world, its results should be viewed cautiously. For instance, the FEMA model is not capable of predicting precise quantitative results, such as the exact level of GNP 20 years after an attack. The results it most reliably produces are qualitative trends, such as the inability of the GNP to recover for decades.

It deserves mention that the computer model used here is not exactly the same as that used in the FEMA report approved for public release in November 1980. Over the last several years, some of the original authors, as well as our group, have worked to fix some of the errors in that program, and have improved its ability to model the U.S. economy.

This report presents the preliminary results of a study that explores the predictive capability of the FEMA simulation program and the degree to which computer modeling can provide reliable predictions of the behavior of the U.S. economy after a nuclear attack. The study was undertaken with several purposes in mind:

A. To determine whether the discrepancy between older static simulation models and the FEMA model is significant in the context of decisions about the nuclear policy of the country.
B. To determine the minimum number of nuclear explosives that would create a perturbation severe enough to collapse the U.S. economy; that is, the number that would be an unquestionable deterrent in the hands of the Soviets. This number, augmented to allow for certainty of delivery, could then become a guideline for future nuclear arms limitation negotiations. For instance, both sides could reduce to a number that would assure them of the ability to deliver the nuclear explosives that would collapse the other side's economy. (FEMA has commissioned a similar computer simulation of the Soviet economy.)
C. To provide a measurement for the efficiency required of a strategic defensive shield designed to permit the U.S. economy to survive a full Soviet nuclear attack.

We have used the FEMA program that simulates the U.S. economy to examine the results of small nuclear attacks that would collapse the U.S. economy. We were looking for the most effective "bottleneck" mechanisms for collapse, and as a consequence we have focused particular attention on liquid fossil fuels. Transportation, energy production, and many crucial industry products depend on liquid fuels. We have found that the shock of denying these resources to the U.S. for even a relatively short period of time disintegrates the economy. This rapid economic deterioration—the "nuclear crash"—could mean that within months of an attack most of the population would starve to death and that the survivors would be reduced to near-medieval levels of existence for decades.

We find that these predictions are not particularly sensitive to the destructiveness assumed for individual attacking weapons. We demonstrate that even using consistently conservative assumptions—which lead to overestimates of the likelihood of a U.S. national economic recovery—an attack consisting of as little as *1% or 2% of the Soviet nuclear arsenal* could cause a complete and long-lasting economic crash in the United States.

At every turn of the research our assumptions, introduced into the computer program either explicitly—as initial values of variables—or implicitly, have been uniformly conservative. We have tested the sensitivity of the computer model over a large range of assumptions, and we present the results of simulation in only those cases when we have biased the assumptions towards recovery of the economy. Yet the perturbations caused by the small, bottlenecking attack scenarios we tested consistently demonstrate the vulnerability of the U.S. economy to a Soviet attack that would not exceed 1% to 2% of their nuclear arsenal.

It bears repeating that the FEMA program we used cannot simulate with high analytical precision the effects of the selective destruction of very small though crucial sectors of the U.S. economy—destruction which we believe would drastically affect the economy. Moreover, limitations exist in any computer model of the economy . . . , and so our results must be read as suggestive rather than definitive. Real nuclear attacks would doubtless be much worse than the FEMA model indicates.

This appendix consists of . . . the most recent information regarding the effects of nuclear explosives on civilian targets. Consistent with our conservative approach we have incorporated into the simulation only two destructive effects, blast and heat, ignoring the effects of the nuclear electromagnetic pulse (EMP) and of delayed radioactive fallout on the U.S. economy. We believe that EMP would in fact have devastating effects on communications and other electronic equipment, including computers, and that fallout would drastically limit the use of undamaged industrial-production capacity and food-producing farm lands, and consequently their inclusion would exacerbate economic dysfunction. But we could not incorporate these effects into the simulation program in a way that would lead to reliable predictions of their impact on the evolution of the economy after the attack.

Then, we consider the effects of three different attack scenarios on the U.S. economy. The first is an attack which destroys 60% of the population and 40% of the industry, which we call the 60/40 Attack. The smallest of the three attacks, the Counter-Energy Attack, destroys only commercial ports and the refining and storage facilities for liquid fossil fuels. The third attack destroys, in addition to the fuel facilities, some key manufacturing sectors such as electronics, primary metals production, and heavy machines. This we call the Counter-Energy Counter-Industry Attack. We present the results in the form of graphs (see Figures B.1 through B.9), with some discussion.

Because of the very large number of assumptions we have necessarily made in exploring the effects of these attacks, two things must be borne firmly in mind when reading this report. First, that the results are uniformly *optimistic*, erring towards the best-case view at every point of choice, and second, that it is *trends* rather than absolute values that one should focus on in reading the report.

Results

In this [section] we will examine the predictions the FEMA model makes for the three base-line attack scenarios: the 60/40 attack (which corresponds to the standard counter-population and counter-industry scenario), the counter-energy attack, and the counter-energy attack augmented with a counter-industry component targeted at key economic sectors like primary metals manufacturing. To test the robustness of the results, we consider a variety of inputs to each of these scenarios.

The Counter-Energy Attack

The counter-energy attack consists of 85 550-kiloton weapons and 154 200-kiloton weapons, a total of 239 nuclear weapons that add up to 110 equivalent megatons—under 2% of the deployed equivalent megatonnage of the Soviet Union. In absolute megatons the attack is even smaller, under 1% of the total Soviet megatons.

The attack is designed to inflict the maximum economic damage while minimizing the attack size; to do this, only the facilities that refine, store and transport liquid fuels are targeted. Although urban areas are not deliberately targeted in this scenario, most of the major U.S. cities end up receiving one or more weapons. This is a by-product of the targeting strategy, which blasts every commercial dock and berth capable of bringing imports into the nation with at least 5 psi.[2] Other explicitly targeted facilities include the nation's Strategic Petroleum Reserve, maintained at five Texas and Louisiana sites by the Department of Energy as a protection against a sudden drop of liquid-fuel availability.[3] Over 95% of all operating U.S. refineries[4] are destroyed by this attack, which also obliterates almost every inactive refinery. The attack targets the major nodes—junctions of over five lines, terminals, and pump or compressor stations—of the nation's three pipeline systems, which are used to transport crude petroleum, petroleum products, and natural gas.[5] Although industrial installations are not selected as targets, the attack also destroys 25% of the nation's primary

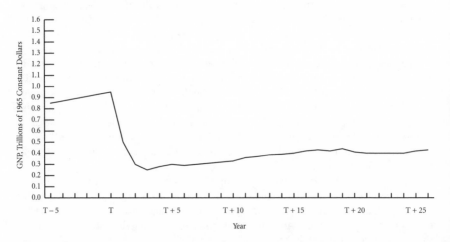

FIGURE B.1   Counter-energy attack: baseline conditions

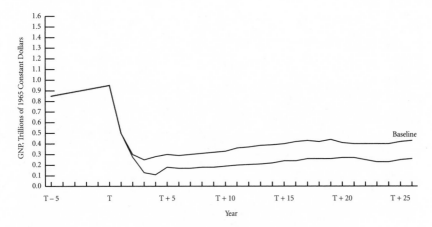

FIGURE B.2   Counter-energy attack: mild psychological effects

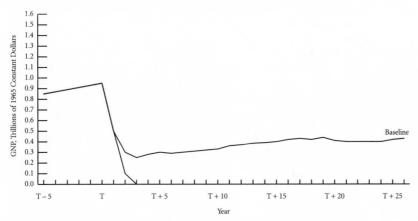

FIGURE B.3   Counter-energy attack: moderate psychological effects

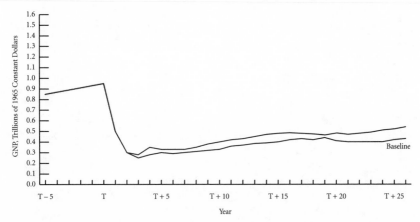

FIGURE B.4   Counter-energy attack: food imports doubled

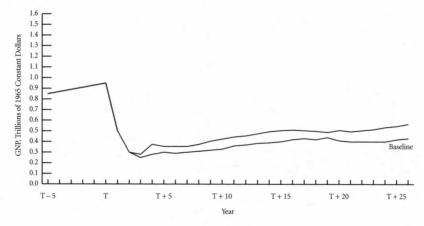

FIGURE B.5   Counter-energy attack: all imports doubled

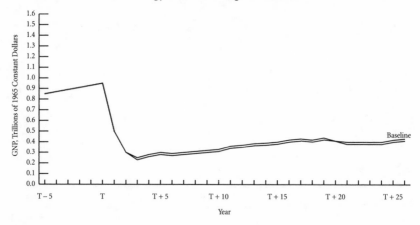

FIGURE B.6   Counter-energy attack: all imports reduced

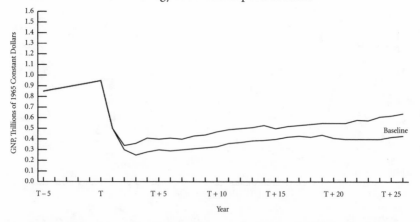

FIGURE B.7   Counter-energy attack: faster rate of transportation reconnection

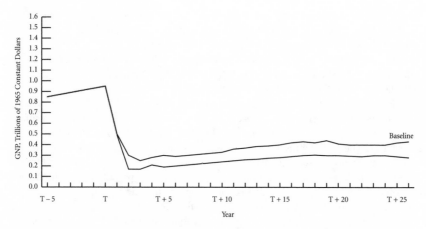

FIGURE B.8   Counter-energy attack: slower rate of transportation reconnection

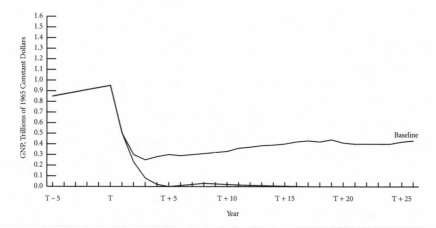

FIGURE B.9   Counter-energy attack: slower rate of transportation reconnection with mild psychological effects

steel manufacturing capacity and 18% of primary nonferrous-metals manufacturing (many
metals-producing plants tend to be located near port and refinery facilities). In all, the U.S.
loses 33% of its capacity to produce energy products, 19% of its capacity to make metals,
and between 5% and 10% of its capacity to manufacture other products; overall, the U.S.
economy loses 8% of its manufacturing capacity. About twenty million Americans die immediately following this attack, which also injures five million: casualties total 10%.

Despite our consistent use of conservative assumptions to estimate damage and casualty
rates, the model simulations indicate that the consequences of the counter-energy attack
would be severe (see figures in this appendix, where we present a representative set of the
graphical output and a discussion of its interpretation). In a scenario that optimistically al-
lows 10% of the pre-attack rate of energy imports and 20% of the pre-attack rate of all other
imports to arrive in the U.S. immediately after the attack (with much higher levels in subse-

quent years—for instance, energy imports double in about one year), includes no psychological effects, and posits that transportation capacity equals demand about one year after the attack, the economy is devastated, as plotted in Figure B.1.

As expected, it is the lack of transportation adequacy that is responsible for the initial plunge in GNP. . . . The attack destroys only 8% of the nation's manufacturing capacity, but GNP falls by over 50% in the first year after the attack.

Available transportation capital falls immediately to about 5% of its pre-attack level. Yet the assumption that transportation capacity equals demand about one year after the attack means in some sense that transportation is no longer a "bottleneck" to recovery one year after the attack. The policy of investment in energy and transportation we have assumed here brings transportation capacity to 50% of its pre-attack level in about one and a half to two years of the attack and brings transportation capacity to near its pre-attack level about three years after the attack. Yet even with these exceedingly optimistic assumptions, the lack of transportation in the early months continues to influence the nation's capacity to produce for decades; for if in these early years people starve and stocks of vital supplies are exhausted, it can take many, many years to undo the harmful effects.

About 8% of the population is killed directly by weapons effects, but almost 60% die within two years of the attack. People starve to death without food, which cannot be transported from the middle of the country where it is produced to the large urban centers on the two coasts, and factories cannot produce goods without materials and labor.

The mass starvation that takes place after this attack (and other attacks) should be considered a qualitative feature of the model. It seems likely to us that the highest priority for the many people in the post-attack world would be survival, rather than rebuilding the U.S. economy. In this case, it is very possible that the U.S. economy would be transformed dramatically after a nuclear attack, perhaps becoming far more agrarian; mass migration to areas near the crop lands of the Midwest might occur. This would allow the land to be cultivated using labor-intensive techniques that do not rely on fossil fuels and machinery. In this way, mass starvation would be avoided. On the other hand, if this occurred, GNP would stabilize at much lower levels than Figure B.1 indicates, and recovery of the GNP to pre-attack levels could take several decades.[6]

To represent people removing themselves from the workforce for any reason (to insure their survival or their family's survival or just because of the psychological shock of the attack), we might include mild psychological effects in the counter-energy attack. The result, indicated in Figure B.2, shows the economy languishing at about a quarter of its pre-attack level for 20 years. It bears repeating that mild psychological effects are rather mild: if the GNP is falling at a rate of 50% per year, the main effect on the economy is that worker productivity falls by a few percent.

Moderate psychological effects have an even more devastating effect on the economy, causing complete economic collapse within three years of the attack, as shown in Figure B.3.

Until the end of the discussion of the counter-energy attack, we will turn off the psychological effects sector of the FEMA model and consider that there is no adverse psychological reaction to the attack. This optimistic assumption will allow us to examine independently the effects of changing the values of other inputs to the model.

Although we consider the level of imports we allot for this attack to be optimistic, we also examine even higher levels of imports. First, we test the original import rates—10% fuel, 20% other goods—augmented by doubling the import availability of food to 40% in just the first year after the attack (as before, these levels are relative to the pre-attack import rates and they are incremented every subsequent year). The results are shown in Figure B.4. GNP is consistently about 15% higher. Fewer people starve, and the economy consequently can perform better. When all imports are doubled, to a rate of 20% for fuel and 40% for other goods, again with higher levels in subsequent years, GNP follows a similar path (see Figure B.5), indicating that it is the food imports that are important. Even higher rates of imports were tested, and while they tended to improve the economy somewhat in the short term, they were not so beneficial in the long term, insofar as they induced the economy to depend on imports, rather than rebuild its own manufacturing base. This is perhaps not surprising, in the light of the events of the past several years.[7]

The conditions represented in the two preceding test runs are probably unrealistically optimistic. Every commercial port that can be used to import significant quantities of goods and materials was destroyed in the counter-energy attack scenario, after all, and every major city targeted. States that had in the past done a great deal of importing would be struggling just to save survivors. Moreover, it is far from clear that other countries will be in a position to help us for they may be struggling in a global depression following the crash of the U.S. economy, or they may be directly targeted (as seems very possible in the case of Canada or Mexico).[8] At the very least, food imports will be very hard to come by after the U.S. stops exporting mass quantities and starts importing. More likely conditions would probably be import rates lower than our baseline rates, with energy imports initially reduced to a trickle, say, 5%. If we permit 15% of all other imports to be brought into the nation, we find that lowering import availability after the counter-energy attack reduces GNP performance only slightly, as shown in Figure B.6.

The transportation reconnection rate turns out to be an important determinant of the recovery rate. Although we consider our baseline conditions optimistic, we consider a policy which results in transportation capacity exceeding demand within months of the attack and has the vast majority of transportation capital returning within two years of the attack. As Figure B.7 shows, GNP is higher and recovery is faster, yet even in this very optimistic case, where the transportation bottleneck lasts less than a year, the economy is devastated and large instabilities threaten recovery.

In Figure B.8 we show the effect of a slower reconnection rate. Here, the prospects for any kind of recovery at all appear bleak. In this case, it takes two years for half of the transportation capital to be reintegrated, at about which time capacity exceeds demand and transportation is no longer a bottleneck to recovery. For many reasons, we believe these assumptions are far more realistic than our baseline conditions.

For instance, an extremely optimistic feature of the model is its assumption that scarce resources are allocated in ways that are optimal to recovery. After a real nuclear war, however, it seems much more likely that scarce resources would be allocated haphazardly (or that the military might simply appropriate them). Therefore, all of the results presented here are already biased towards predictions of recovery in situations that in reality could cause the immediate downward plunge of GNP characteristic of complete collapse. Yet our simulations that show GNP stagnating at levels a small fraction of pre-attack GNP cannot be considered recovery; indeed, one of the few things we can be fairly confident about in such cases is that the economy is not recovering.

As we have said, our baseline conditions combine several assumptions we believe to be optimistic. If we made just two of those assumptions more realistic—adding mild psychological effects to the slower recommendation rate for transportation—the counter-energy attack collapses the economy, as shown in Figure B.9. As before, transportation capacity exceeds demand within two years, yet by this time the population has dwindled and incentives to increase the recovery simply do not work: the survivors are discouraged. In the second post-attack decade, as the anticipated recovery fails to materialize, public confidence plunges further and workers begin to withdraw from the organized economy, possibly to take part in fractionalized, low-level forms of economic activity. It is this migration that finally causes the complete collapse of the U.S. economy.

This is perhaps the most realistic path for the economy after the counter-energy attack.

Source

Program in Science and Technology for International Security, M.I.T. 20A–001 Cambridge, MA 02139; Report #17, June 1987.

APPENDIX C:
CALCULATION OF RUSSIAN FORCES SURVIVING A
U.S. PREEMPTIVE ATTACK

TABLE C.1   3,000 Russian Warheads

Number	Type Weapon	Percent Attrition	Number Surviving
300	Fixed ICBMs	90	30
300	Mobile ICBMs	50	150
800	SLBMs at sea	50	400
800	SLBMs in port	90	80
800	ALCMs on bombers	50	400
Total 3,000		Total surviving U.S. attack	1,060

Attrition of the surviving 1,060 Russian Warheads
while conducting retaliatory attacks on the United States

Type Attrition	Percent Attrition	Number Surviving
Friction		
180 ICBMs	10	162
480 SLBMs	10	432
400 ALCMs	10	360
Ballistic Missile Defense		
Versus 162 ICBMs	70	49
Versus 432 SLBMs	70	130
Other defenses versus 360 ALCMs	0	360
	Total penetrating to United States	539

Alternative calculation of attrition of 1,060 warheads during attack

Type Attrition	Percent Attrition	Number Surviving
Friction		
180 ICBMs	10	162
480 SLBMs	10	432
400 ALCMs	10	360
Ballistic Missile Defense		
Versus 162 ICBMs	90	16
Versus 432 SLBMs	90	43
Other defenses versus 360 ALCMs	0	360
	Total penetrating to United States	419

Second alternative calculation of attrition of 1,060 warheads during attack

Type Attrition	Percent Attrition	Number Surviving
Friction		
180 ICBMs	50	90
480 SLBMs	50	240
400 ALCMs	50	200
Ballistic Missile Defense		
Versus 90 ICBMs	90	9
Versus 240 SLBMs	90	24
Other defenses versus 200 ALCMs	0	200
	Total penetrating to United States	233

TABLE C.2   1,000 Russian Warheads (Same percentages by weapon type as Case 1)

Number	Type Weapon	Percent Attrition	Number Surviving
100	Fixed ICBMs	90	10
100	Mobile ICBMs	50	50
266	SLBMs at sea	50	133
266	SLBMs in port	90	27
268	ALCMs on bombers	50	134
Total 1,000		Total surviving U.S. attack	354

*Attrition of the surviving 354 Russian Warheads
while conducting retaliatory attacks on the United States*

Type Attrition	Percent Attrition	Number Surviving
Friction		
60 ICBMs	10	54
160 SLBMs	10	144
134 ALCMs	10	120
Ballistic Missile Defense		
Versus 54 ICBMs	70	16
Versus 144 SLBMs	70	43
Other defenses versus 120 ALCMs	0	120
	Total penetrating to United States	179

Alternative calculation of attrition of 354 warheads during attack

Type Attrition	Percent Attrition	Number Surviving
Friction		
60 ICBMs	10	54
160 SLBMs	10	144
134 ALCMs	10	120
Ballistic Missile Defense		
Versus 54 ICBMs	90	5
Versus 144 SLBMs	90	14
Other defenses versus 120 ALCMs	0	120
	Total penetrating to United States	139

Second alternative calculation of attrition of 354 warheads during attack

Type Attrition	Percent Attrition	Number Surviving
Friction		
60 ICBMs	50	30
160 SLBMs	50	80
134 ALCMs	50	67
Ballistic Missile Defense		
Versus 30 ICBMs	90	3
Versus 80 SLBMs	90	8
Other defenses versus 66 ALCMs	0	67
	Total Penetrating to United States	78

148

TABLE C.3   250 Russian Warheads (Same percentages by weapon type as Case 1)

Number	Type Weapon	Percent Attrition	Number Surviving
25	Fixed ICBMs	90	3
25	Mobile ICBMs	50	13
66	SLBMs at sea	50	33
66	SLBMs in port	90	7
68	ALCMs on bombers	50	34
Total 250		Total surviving U.S. attack	90

Attrition of the surviving 90 Russian Warheads
while conducting retaliatory attacks on the United States

Type Attrition	Percent Attrition	Number Surviving
Friction		
16 ICBMs	10	14
40 SLBMs	10	36
34 ALCMs	10	30
Ballistic Missile Defense		
Versus 14 ICBMs	70	4
Versus 36 SLBMs	70	11
Other defenses versus 30 ALCMs	0	30
	Total penetrating to United States	45

Alternative calculation of attrition of 90 warheads during attack

Type Attrition	Percent Attrition	Number Surviving
Friction		
16 ICBMs	10	14
40 SLBMs	10	36
34 ALCMs	10	30
Ballistic Missile Defense		
Versus 14 ICBMs	90	1
Versus 36 SLBMs	90	4
Other defenses versus 30 ALCMs	0	30
	Total penetrating to United States	35

(continues)

Second alternative calculation of attrition of 90 warheads during attack

Type Attrition	Percent Attrition	Number Surviving
Friction		
16 ICBMs	50	8
40 SLBMs	50	20
34 ALCMs	50	17
Ballistic Missile Defense		
Versus 8 ICBMs	90	1
Versus 20 SLBMs	90	2
Other defenses versus 17 ALCMs	0	17
	Total penetrating to United States	20

TABLE C.4   250 Russian Warheads (Percentages of weapons adjusted to emphasize invulnerability and cruise missiles)

Number	Type Weapon	Percent Attrition	Number Surviving
50	Mobile ICBMs	50	25
50	SLBMs at sea	50	25
50	SLBMs in port	90	5
100	ALCMs on bombers	50	50
Total 250		Total surviving U.S. attack	105

Attrition of the surviving 105 Russian Warheads
while conducting retaliatory attacks on the United States

Type Attrition	Percent Attrition	Number Surviving
Friction		
25 ICBMs	50	13
30 SLBMs	50	15
50 ALCMs	50	25
Ballistic Missile Defense		
Versus 13 ICBMs	90	1
Versus 15 SLBMs	90	2
Other defenses versus 25 ALCMs	0	25
	Total penetrating to United States	28

Notes

Chapter One

1. Nuclear blast effects are measured in the weight of TNT that would release the same amount of energy. Because the numbers are so large, the standard measure of "yield" is in metric tonnes of TNT; to abbreviate further we talk of thousands of tonnes or kilotons (KT); or even millions of tonnes (MT). The sum of the explosive power of the 32,500 warheads in our peak inventory in 1967 was just more than 12,500 MT.

12,500 × 1,000,000 tonnes/MT = 12,500,000,000 tonnes.
12,500,000,000 × 2,200 lbs./tonne = 27,500,000,000,000 lbs.
27,500,000,000,000 lbs./500 lbs./bomb = 55,000,000,000 bombs.

This is not to say that 55 billion 500-pound bombs and 32,500 nuclear warheads that summed up to 12,500 MT would do identical damage; only to indicate a rough magnitude of comparison.

2. The Hiroshima bomb is estimated to have had a yield of 12.5 KT or 12,500 tonnes. The estimated total explosive power of our 32,500 warheads in 1967 was at 12,500 MT or 12,500,000,000 tonnes. That total divided by the 12,500 tonnes at Hiroshima is 1,000,000 Hiroshima-sized bombs.

3. Mark Selden, "The United States, Japan, and the Atomic Bomb," *Bulletin of Concerned Asian Scholars*, Vol. 23, No. 1 (January–March 1991), p. 7.

4. Richard Halloran, "Weinberger Angered by Reports on War Strategy," *New York Times*, August 24, 1982, p. B8.

5. Robert W. Tucker, "The Nuclear Debate," *Foreign Affairs* (Fall 1984), p. 9.

6. Lawrence Freedman, "I Exist: Therefore I Deter," *International Security*, Vol. 13, No. 1 (Summer 1988), p. 179.

7. Ibid., p. 182.

8. "Supreme Commander Pessimistic on Defense Building" (Interview with Karen Elliott House and Gerald F. Seib), *Wall Street Journal*, June 5, 1984, p. 38.

9. Author interview with Zbigniew Brzezinski, November 1996; and Robert M. Gates, *From the Shadows* (New York: Simon and Schuster, 1996), pp. 113–115.

10. Shaun Gregory, *Hidden Cost of Deterrence: Nuclear Weapons Accidents* (London: Brassey's, 1990), p. 96.

11. Melinda Lamont-Havers, *Estimated Nuclear Weapons Stockpiles, 1990–2003* (Washington, D.C.: Coalition to Reduce Nuclear Dangers, January 1997).

12. From the testimony of Dr. Bruce G. Blair, senior fellow in foreign policy studies at the Brookings Institution, before the U.S. House National Security Committee, March 13, 1997.

13. *Nuclear News*, February 28–March 13, 1996.

Day	Washington Post	New York Times
February 28	UN/Iraq weapons inspection China/Pakistan proliferation threat	OpEd, China's strategic position OpEd, Euratom, proliferation TV review (PBS)
February 29	DOE plans (United States) DOE plans (Russia)	Export licenses/China DOE plans (United States)
March 1	German Spy Chief (Plutonium planting) GOP debate	Forbes foreign policy
March 5	Chinese rocket (Intelsat) Clinton defense budget	China missile tests off Taiwan
March 6	OpEd, future of disarmament Pakistan nuclear test plans China missile tests off Taiwan Documents reveal atomic spy	Documents reveal atomic spy
March 7	DOD BMD plans China missile tests off Taiwan	China missile tests off Taiwan
March 8	Debt limit, U.S. Uranium Enrichment Corp. Secretary O'Leary, nuclear testing Chinese missile tests off Taiwan China supplies Iran with gas technology Chess in Baghdad, UN sanctions	Congress to kill one agency of three Chinese missile tests off Taiwan Russia to support CTBT
March 11	China missile tests off Taiwan Citizens Advisory Panel on BMD UN inspection in Baghdad	UN inspection in Baghdad
March 12	UN inspection in Baghdad China warns United States (missile tests) U.S. sends second carrier (missile tests)	U.S. policy on Taiwan (missile tests) China warns U.S. (missile tests) UN inspection in Baghdad OpEd, China missile tests Hong Kong stocks (missile tests) Collapse of Sovietology
March 13	Nuclear waste plant opens Chinese exercises (missile tests)	Nuclear waste plant opens Russian proliferation threat Chinese exercises (missile tests)

Chapter Two

1. The Director of Central Intelligence coordinates the twelve organizations that together make up the U.S. Intelligence Community and also heads one of those, the Central Intelligence Agency (CIA).

2. Richard P. Hallion, *Storm Over Iraq* (Washington, D.C.: Smithsonian Institution Press, 1992), p. 188.

3. U.S. Congress, Office of Technology Assessment, *The Effects of Nuclear War* (Washington, D.C.: Government Printing Office, 1979), p. 22.

4. Yuri M. Shcherbak, "Ten Years of the Chernobyl Era," *Scientific American,* April 1, 1996, pp. 44–49.

5. David A. Rosenberg, "The Origins of Overkill," *International Security*, Vol. 7, No. 4 (Spring 1983), p. 55.

6. Carl von Clausewitz, *On War*, Ed. and Trans. Michael Howard and Peter Paret (Princeton: Princeton University Press, 1976), p. 230.

7. Fred Kaplan, *The Wizards of Armageddon* (Stanford: Stanford University Press, 1983), p. 269.

8. Alain Enthoven, as quoted in ibid., p. 254.

9. William J. Broad, "Economic Collapse Tied to Atom War," *New York Times*, June 26, 1987, p. 1.

10. Office of Technology Assessment, *The Effects of Nuclear War*, p. 21.

11. I am indebted on this point to McGeorge Bundy's excellent and thorough analysis of the Berlin crisis in his *Danger and Survival* (New York: Vintage Books, 1990), pp. 378–383.

Chapter Three

1. Carl von Clausewitz, *On War*, Ed. and Trans. Michael Howard and Peter Paret (Princeton: Princeton University Press, 1976), p. 67.

2. Colin Powell with Joseph E. Persico, *My American Journey* (New York: Random House, 1995), p. 486.

Chapter Four

1. Central Intelligence Agency, "Soviet Civil Defense," NI 78-1003, July 1978, p. 2.

2. Richard Ned Lebow, *Nuclear Crisis Management—A Dangerous Illusion* (Ithaca: Cornell University Press, 1987), p. 84.

3. McGeorge Bundy, *Danger and Survival* (New York: Vintage Books, 1990), pp. 605–606.

Chapter Five

1. I am indebted to Alton Frye for this term. See his "Banning Ballistic Missiles," *Foreign Affairs* (November/December 1996), p. 103.

Chapter Six

1. This was first enunciated by the U.S. representatives at the North Atlantic Council meeting in November 1991.
2. Charles de Gaulle, "Discours et messages," cited in McGeorge Bundy, *Danger and Survival* (New York: Vintage Books, 1990), pp. 4–73.

Chapter Seven

1. Joseph Cirincione, "Why the Right Lost the Missile Defense Debate," *Foreign Policy* (Spring 1997), p. 39.
2. R. W. Apple Jr., "Scud Missile Hits U.S. Barracks, Killing 27," *New York Times*, February 26, 1991, p. A-1.
3. George N. Lewis and Theodore A. Postol, "Video Evidence on the Effectiveness of Patriot During the 1991 Gulf War," *Science and Global Security*, Vol. 4. (1993), pp. 1–63.
4. This scenario is suggested in Bruce G. Blair, "Controls and Alert Rates of Missiles," in *The Last 15 Minutes: Ballistic Missile Defense in Perspective,* Ed. Joseph Cirincione and Frank von Hippel (Washington, D.C.: Coalition to Reduce Nuclear Dangers, 1996), p. 35.
5. In the current conditions in Russia, its strategic forces are not being maintained in the most survivable mode, i.e., a large percentage of submarines at sea and mobile missiles on the road. We must assume, however, that in any period of nuclear tensions they would be. But we should also remember that even one or two Russian submarines at sea would almost certainly evade destruction and would carry a potent retaliation.

Chapter Eight

1. "Report of the Canberra Commission on the Elimination of Nuclear Weapons" (Canberra, Australia: National Capital Printers, August 1996), Executive Summary at p. 7.

Chapter Nine

1. Janne Nolan, *Guardians of the Arsenal* (New York: Basic Books, 1989), p. 57.
2. Author's interview with Admiral Elmo R. Zumwalt, a member of the Joint Chiefs of Staff at that time.
3. Carl von Clausewitz, *On War*, Ed. and Trans. Michael Howard and Peter Paret (Princeton: Princeton University Press, 1976), p. 606.

Appendix A

1. U.S. Congress, Senate Foreign Relations Committee, March 1974, p. 26, cited in *The Medical Implications of Nuclear War* (Washington, D.C.: National Academy Press, 1986), p. 219.
2. Ibid., p. 220.
3. Kosta Tsipis, *Arsenal* (New York: Simon and Schuster, 1983), p. 44 (data extrapolated).

4. Richard P. Hallion, *Storm over Iraq* (Washington, D.C.: Smithsonian Institution Press, 1992), p. 188.

5. Theodore Postol, "Nuclear War: Effects of Nuclear Weapons," in *The Encyclopedia of Americana*, international ed., vol. 20 (Danbury, Conn.: Grolier, 1990), p. 519.

6. U.S. Congress, Office of Technology Assessment, *The Effects of Nuclear War* (Washington, D.C.: Government Printing Office, 1979), p. 16.

7. William Daugherty, Barbara Leir, and Frank von Hippel, "The Consequences of 'Limited' Nuclear Attacks on the United States," *International Security*, Vol. 10, No. 4 (Spring 1986), p. 19.

8. Theodore Postol, "Possible Fatalities from Superfires Following Nuclear Attacks in or Near Urban Areas," in *Medical Implications of Nuclear War*, p. 65.

9. Office of Technology Assessment, *The Effects of Nuclear War*, p. 21.

10. J. Carson Mark, *The Final Epidemic* (Chicago: Educational Foundation for Nuclear Science, 1981), p. 98.

11. Thesis enunciated by T. K. Jones, deputy undersecretary of defense for strategic and theater nuclear forces, as cited in Robert Scheer, *With Enough Shovels* (New York: Random House, 1982).

12. Daugherty, Leir, and von Hippel, "The Consequences of 'Limited' Nuclear Attacks on the United States," p. 19.

13. Steve Fetter and Kosta Tsipis, "Catastrophic Nuclear Radiation Releases," Program in Science and Technology for International Security, Report No. 5, MIT, Cambridge, Massachusetts, September 1980, p. 17.

14. Robert Ehrlich, *Waging Nuclear Peace: The Technology and Politics of Nuclear Weapons* (Albany: State University of New York, 1985), p. 174.

Appendix B

1. Of the extensive literature on this subject, these are the works we referred to most: S. Glasstone and P. Dolan, eds., *The Effects of Nuclear Weapons*, Government Printing Office, 1977; Congressional Office of Technology Assessment (OTA), *The Effects of Nuclear War*, Government Printing Office, 1979; Arms Control and Disarmament Agency (ACDA), *An Analysis of Civil Defense in Nuclear War*, 1978; W. Daugherty, B. Levi, and F. von Hippel, "The Consequences of 'Limited' Nuclear Attacks on the United States," *International Security*, Spring, 1986; T. Postol, *Possible Fatalities from Superfires Following Nuclear Attacks in or Near Urban Areas*, paper presented at the Institute of Medicine's Symposium on the Medical Effects of Nuclear War, National Academy of Sciences, Washington, D.C., September 20–22, 1985; AMBIO, Nuclear War: The Aftermath, Volume XI, Number 2–3, 1985; A. M. Katz, *Life After Nuclear War*, Ballinger, 1982; R. Goen, R. Bothun, and F. Walker, *Potential Vulnerability Affecting National Survival* (PVANS), Stanford Research Institute (SRI), September 1970; F. Dresch and S. Baum, *Analysis of the U.S. and USSR Potential for Economic Recovery Following A Nuclear Attack*, Stanford Research Institute, 1973; Economic Model commissioned by Federal Emergency Management Agency as described in *Development of a Dynamic Model to Evaluate Economic Recovery Following a Nuclear Attack, Final Report, Volume I: Description and Simulations*, November 1980, Pugh-Roberts Associates, Inc., Cambridge, MA.

2. Water Resources Support Center, U.S. Corps of Engineers, *Port Series*, Government Printing Office, 1983–84.

3. Assistant Secretary for Fossil Energy, Department of Energy, *Strategic Petroleum Reserve: Annual Report*, Government Printing Office, 1984. R.G. Lawson, "Strategic Petroleum Construction Ends First Phase," *Oil and Gas Journal*, 21 July 1980.

4. Aileen Cantrell, "Annual Refining Survey," *Oil and Gas Journal*, March 1983, 1984, and 1985.

5. Penn Well Maps, *Product Pipelines of the United States and Canada*, Penn Well Publishing, 1983; *Crude Oil Pipelines of the United States and Canada*, Penn Well Publishing, 1982; *Natural Gas Pipelines of the United States and Canada*, Penn Well Publishing, 1982.

6. As discussed previously, this happened to some extent in both Japan and Germany after World War II.

7. Imports cannot be relied on forever. If imports become an external crutch for the U.S. economy, then the internal rebuilding process can be slowed down, which can seriously hurt the long-term prospects for the economy.

8. As we have said before, if the point of the attack is to collapse the U.S. economy and keep it from recovering, the Soviets might well target a few weapons on Canada and Mexico to put them in no position to aid the United States, at least in the short term when it is the most critical.

ABOUT THE BOOK AND AUTHOR

The Cold War may be over, but you wouldn't know it from the tens of thousands of nuclear weapons still held by Russia and the United States. Arguing that the time has come to dispense with incremental approaches to arms control, Admiral Stansfield Turner, the former head of the CIA and an experienced senior military commander, proposes a practical yet safe plan that would move the world into a new and secure millennium.

First, Turner carefully analyzes how many nuclear weapons are really needed to maintain our national security, regardless of how many weapons of mass destruction other nations may have. He then offers a dramatic, unilateral American initiative—to place all of the world's nuclear warheads in "strategic escrow" whereby none would be ready for immediate use; to initiate a pledge of "no first-use" and call on other nations to do the same; and to build national defenses against nuclear attacks when they become cost-effective.

The Turner Plan achieves genuine international security and has the potential to receive wide, bipartisan support. It deserves to be widely studied, debated, and, finally, implemented.

INDEX

ABM. *See* Anti-Ballistic Missile Treaty
Accidents, 18, 53, 54, 110
Acheson-Lilienthal/Baruch plan, 108
ADMs. *See* Atomic demolition munitions
Afghanistan, 1, 76, 99, 103
Akhromeyev, Sergei, 49, 65–66, 72
Alerts. *See* Nuclear alerts
Anti-Ballistic Missile (ABM) Treaty, 86, 88, 91
Arms control, 21, 33, 71, 79, 97, 110, 118(n). *See also individual treaties*
Arms Control and Disarmament Agency, 114, 122
Atomic demolition munitions (ADMs), 74–75
Australia, 101

Baker, James, 46
Ballistic Missile Early Warning System, 85
Belarus, 21, 72(n), 77
Berlin crises (1958/1963), 40, 43
Black market, 22
Bombers, 18, 29, 57, 58, 89, 90, 113, 115, 118, 126. *See also* Strategic Air Command
Border surveillance, 93–94
Brenner Pass, 74, 75
Brezhnev, Leonid, 97
Brzezinski, Zbigniew, 17, 98, 99, 108
Bulgaria, 8
Bundy, McGeorge, 58–59
Bureaucracies, 110, 113, 114, 116
Bush, George, 47, 65, 66, 68, 109, 110
Butler, Lee, 10, 118

California, 143
Canada, 76, 143, 155(n8)

Canberra Commission on the Elimination of Nuclear Weapons, 101
Carter, Jimmy, 17, 97, 99, 107, 108, 109, 110
Carthage, 32, 52, 104
Casualties. *See* Deaths
Central Intelligence Agency (CIA), 27, 28, 42, 51–52, 107, 114, 117. *See also* Intelligence issues
Chaos/complexity theory, 36(n)
Chechnya, 71, 76
Chemical/biological weapons, 34, 45, 46, 48, 104
Cheney, Dick, 109
Chernobyl, 30, 129
China, 19, 20, 23, 34, 39, 48, 55, 62, 79, 100
    non-recovery point in, 37–38, 102–103, 112
    nuclear capability, 37–38, 70, 77, 86, 94
    self-deterrence point, 49–50
CIA. *See* Central Intelligence Agency
Civil defense, 51, 52, 130. *See also* Defenses
Clausewitz, Carl von, 34, 43, 88, 110–111
Clinton, Bill, 23, 110
Cold War, 20–21, 24, 44, 61, 76, 98, 99, 100, 103, 110, 120, 121, 122
Communications, 59, 130, 132. *See also* Electromagnetic pulse
Comprehensive Test Ban Treaty (CTBT), 23
Conference Board, 51
Controlled response doctrine, 60–61, 111, 112, 113
Conventional weapons/forces, 12, 14, 19, 22, 29, 44, 46, 47, 48–49, 55, 57, 76, 77, 80, 82, 82(n), 113, 114
    conventional war, 13, 39, 60, 76, 77, 85, 104, 106

157

NATIONAL UNIVERSITY LIBRARY SAN DIEGO